CHASING
SHADOWS

A Criminal Investigator's
Look into the Paranormal

CHASING
SHADOWS

A Criminal Investigator's Look into the Paranormal

Mark Allan Keyes

As featured on Discovery's *The Haunted*, co-star of *Surviving Evidence* and host of WILK's *Paranormal Science*

Rowe Publishing

ISBN 13: 978-1-939054-35-7
ISBN 10: 1-939054-35-4

Cover photos of author by BREYNOLDS Photography.

This is a work of nonfiction, however, to protect the privacy of those involved, names, locations, and/or dates have been changed, and composite characters were created when necessary.

1 3 5 7 9 8 6 4 2

Printed in the United States of America
Published by

Rowe Publishing

www.rowepub.com
Stockton, Kansas

To my best friend...
my wife, Lauren

For sacrificing so much of our personal time that we could have been together and for sharing me with the universe so I could pursue my dreams, I love you!

For helping me create an incredible paranormal research team which, in turn, has helped so many people in so many ways, I thank you!

If there are angels watching over us, I am certain they sent me you!

Foreword

Sometimes one never knows when we'll meet someone who will have a tremendous impact on our lives, and often those days arrive unexpectedly and without much fanfare. Yet as that day comes and passes, we remember the details with remarkable clarity. The day I met Mark Keyes was one such day.

I was on the set of, *Surviving Evidence*, a movie about Chris DiCesare who had endured a malevolent haunting while in college. Though the story was certainly not a happy one, this amazing and wonderfully humble man walked away from a rather harrowing experience thinking this 'ghost' that taunted him, attacked him, threatened his inner peace, and outer reputation had no true malice in its intent. To me, who comes into the realm of paranormal in ways that were rather peaceful and even loving, I saw Chris as an Angel on Earth. In the film, I portrayed a malevolent spirit, and while on set, I met Mark Keyes who was there to play an investigator that, for the sake of the film, wasn't buying into Chris' story. The film, meant as the second film about Chris and his story, at the time of this writing is slated for release as part of an updated version to their previous film entitled *Please, Talk With Me* in their Anniversary Edition marking 30 years since the haunting took place.

When I first met Mark I learned he worked for the State Police, and I thanked him for his service. To me, both as a parent and as someone who is lucky enough to live in a community where we can walk the streets at night, I have had a tremendous respect for those in law enforcement. After all, they risk their lives to keep our communities safer.

I've had several opportunities to talk with Officers local to me about some of the things that haunt them, away from 'ghosts', and hearing the stories of what keeps these brave folks up nights gave me an even higher respect for them. Yet there are some Officers, though relatively few, who do have some sense for the paranormal. Those I've met that are into paranormal and metaphysical seem to be as much in service to these realms as they are in service to us, and in mine eyes they are twice remarkable for that.

Mark has established a place in one of my life's finest happenings. I was writing a book, which would tell of my experiences when attuned as a spirit medium. Originally intended as a nonfiction, my years working in paranormal talk radio had shown me that the more I represent myself as a medium, the more people will want 'the circus act', in other words, daring me to show and prove my acumen to them based on whoever died around them, and to me it simply doesn't work that way. So instead, I decided to write a fiction work, where the central character is a spirit medium. Long story short, I had gotten to Chapter 7 before reaching a total blank... so I put the work aside hoping for something inspire me.

That day arrived when, as fortune would have it, I had Mark Keyes on as a guest for a radio show I hosted, called *Beyond the Norm*. Mark was telling of how he and a team of other law enforcement officers were working to pacify malevolent hauntings in his local communities, and this team would not move on to the next case until their clients were pacified.

I had never heard of such a thing. There is a show on TV, one of my personal favorites called The Dead Files, and in that show there is a retired homicide detective named Steve DiSchiavi and a spirit medium named Amy Allan. These two visit some of the worst malevolent haunting locations in the country. Steve investigates the history of the property, finding any and all information about who may have died on or near the property, or what terrible events may have occurred near there. Amy gets information using her incredible gift as a spirit medium, and together they compare notes for the clients, and advise the clients as to what measures they could take to rid the property of malevolence. They do a tremendously good job, but they have a very busy production schedule obligating them to move onto the next case…whereas Mark's team has the benefit of being there for their clients until the job is finished and I thought that quite amazing.

While interviewing Mark on the radio show, I asked him which is worse in his findings…the living or the dead? I thought it a great question! Without hesitation or doubt, he had a clear answer…the living. They are capable of the most deprived behaviors toward other living people, and Mark has seen firsthand some horrid things…things that you or I likely wouldn't be able to handle or deal with, and Mark sees them often day after day. I still find it hard to imagine what that must be like.

When the radio interview was over, I had found a new hero, and it was enough to not only inspire a return to writing my book, but it even introduced a new character…a Homicide Detective, a character that worked perfectly into the story. I started writing the book over from scratch and finished within three days!

All the books I have read over the years that had to do with the paranormal, I believe that *Chasing Shadows* is truly best among them. Believe me, I have read a lot of books on the subject from many of the greatest minds and personalities in the paranormal realm, and between that and hosting radio shows on the subject, had read through even more, and I believe myself quite qualified to enter that opinion. I'm honored to write the Foreword for this book.

So I will conclude with this. Mark provides a fantastic perspective of seeing paranormal activity through the eyes and mind of someone very well trained to notice things in his surrounding environment, differing things between perception and belief, and the stringent standard it requires to pass the test to make it beyond simple skepticism. The process Mark gives throughout this book is fascinating, very well conveyed, and makes for one of the most compelling books I'd ever read on any subject, let alone a subject I've spent over three decades tantalized by. Ghosts, paranormal, metaphysics, law enforcement, and the human experience are all part of *Chasing Shadows*.

I hope you will agree, that this is one of the finest books you will ever read on this subject.

Chip Reichenthal
Author of *Even the Dead Won't Tell You the Truth*
Radio Host, A1B; Art Bell *Dark Matter*

Introduction

The question is, "Are ghosts real?" I would tell you, but it's really up to you to figure out for yourself! In the words of the great, late physicist, Albert Einstein... "Hello!"

Ok, I'm just being funny, of course, but he is one of my favorites and probably did say that on more than one occasion. Allow me to introduce myself. Born into a middle class family in rural Pennsylvania, I was honored with the name of Mark Allan Keyes. By all accounts, I was a normal child growing up. Well, depending upon who you ask and what your idea of normal is. My parents divorced when I was ten years old and I was raised by my mother, with a younger brother and sister to torment. Being the oldest of three children, much of the responsibility of taking care of our home fell into my hands so that our mother could work. One thing about being raised by a single parent is that you gain much more responsibility quickly, or at least I did.

As I look back on it, there was great value through that experience and it taught me how to think for myself. I like to believe that I was somewhere near the top of the "average intelligence" scale, but really could have applied myself more. The fact was, I was more of a hands-on type of kid and liked to daydream, although

I thought science was kind of cool while going through my school years. I liked to poke at things and science sometimes provided me a chance to do that. But for the most part, sitting in a classroom all day, listening to a teacher rehash what I could read in a book was simply boring to me. I felt restrained in school and couldn't wait to get out and get moving.

I liked to be outside as much as possible. When I was inside, I was usually watching TV. Yes, I was a very big fan of TV, which back then was much like the Internet is today for a kid when it came to learning new things outside of school. If there was something on that dealt with superheroes or the supernatural, I was watching it. I also loved anything to do with emergency services. Cops and firemen were just as much superheroes to me as Superman or the Green Lantern. Roy DeSoto and Jonny Gage from a TV show called *Emergency*, which aired in the 70s, were two of my biggest heroes. After watching them, one thing was for sure, a nine-to-five desk job was not for me. I needed to save people and be anywhere the action was. So, while I sat in class, my thoughts were focused on things like being a fireman, police officer, or a fighter pilot. I wanted to make a difference!

After I did my time in school, I went on to Wilkes University where I earned a Bachelor's degree in Psychology, became a volunteer fireman and EMT, worked as a Deputy Officer with the Pennsylvania Fish and Boat Commission Bureau of Law Enforcement, all while working as a full-time 911 dispatcher. It gave me something to do! I was where the action was and loving every minute of it. I later enlisted with the State Police, where I have held various positions along the way, including an assignment as undercover narcotics investigator for 10 years. Those years were filled with such crazy experiences that it would fill another book.

I finally came to rest as a criminal investigator for the last few years of my career. Most people would be more familiar with the term "Detective," but that unit's function was to investigate major crimes such as sexual assaults, robberies, suicides, or other non-natural deaths and homicides.

As I write this book, I am forty-four years old, have a beautiful wife named Lauren, three great children, and now have less than four years to retirement that will end a wonderful twenty-five-year career. Two things I can say I have learned from working as a Trooper for so long, dead people freak me out (but not the way you think) and the living are far scarier than the dead. I've had a great life so far, with typical ups and downs, and a very satisfying career that I can say I am proud of. However, something happened along the way. I heard a voice. Literally! And not just once! It started me on a search for answers and I had no idea where the Universe was about to take me.

Chapter 1

Who's There?

Did you ever get the feeling that you're not alone? If so, then you might understand where I'm coming from. Imagine being twelve years old, alone in the backyard of your rural home, cutting grass with no one else around, and someone yells your name. No big deal, right? It happens all the time. Somebody is trying to get your attention and the sound of the mower is drowning out their voice. So they yell your name to grab your attention. You turn around to see what they want and, surprise, there's no one there. Okay, so that's a little unusual. This unusual experience made it all the way to becoming a line in a movie, but more on that later!

I still look back and remember it as if it were yesterday. There I was, a preteen boy with a pile of responsibilities, including cutting the grass. The thing was, I loved cutting the grass. Under all that motor noise was my quiet time, my time to think. We had a large yard and an old push mower, but when you put the two together, it gave me plenty of time to reflect on my short life and big dreams. It sounds odd, but I can remember having two sided conversations with myself about all kinds of things. I would ask questions and answer them in my head. It was like weighing my options and debating my plans with another person, but by myself, in my own head. I would completely lose myself in thought and the rest of the world would disappear as I daydreamed my work away.

Looking back now, after all I have learned about the metaphysical world, cutting grass became a time of meditation for me, although I had no idea that I was doing it then. So, the big question was, and the big question that still remains is... Who called my name? There was no one there. It wasn't a case of ambient noise mixed with lawn mower sound to create a mistaken impression of someone calling my name, and it definitely wasn't an unknown sound wherein I thought that maybe someone called my name, but wasn't sure. This was loud and clear, a distinct male voice, and right behind me. I jumped when I heard it because the voice was so close and unexpectedly loud. I became a little freaked out, I must admit, when I turned and found nobody standing there. Only being about a half-an-hour into a two-hour grass-cutting day, I now had a lot more to think about.

I've had the opportunity to do many public appearances and lecture on my experiences with the paranormal over the years. The number one most asked question I receive from people is, how did I get involved in paranormal research? It's a question that I have asked of people in that field many times myself. Most people report having encounters with ghosts or living in a home that they believe was haunted and later want to continue exploring those experiences. I never saw a ghost, I never lived in a haunted house, and I never personally knew anyone who did, or at least knew someone who wasn't afraid to admit that they did. When I was growing up, people would have called you crazy for claiming you saw a ghost. The only thing I knew about ghosts was what I saw on TV or in the movies, and they were mostly portrayed in a negative light. The single motivating event that piqued my interest in paranormal research goes back to an experience of a twelve-year-old boy hearing a simple voice and asking the question... "Who's there?" This event left such an impression on me that I still carry it with me today as strongly as when I first asked the question. The reason behind this is that I still don't know the answer to the question.

When I first had this experience, like any person, I tried to make logical sense of it. I came up with a few ideas of what I thought it may have been and, ultimately, threw my hands up in surrender and admitted I had no idea if it was real or just something I imagined. Was it all in my head? Did I have a psychic experience while in some state of meditation? Was it a voice from beyond of someone lurking in my backyard trying to reach out to me? If that were the case, it made me feel a little uneasy because it knew my name, whoever "it" was. Having worked with so many psychic mediums in this field and asking their opinion, the majority of them believe it may have been a spirit guide calling for me. The key word being *may*! To a criminal investigator, the word may leaves the door wide open for other possibilities. So, for a short period of time, I started paying closer attention to TV shows and books that had anything to do with ghosts or extra sensory perception (ESP).

Time went on as life took over and the thoughts of what had taken place were replaced with a million other teenage priorities that consumed my attention, but every now and then, something would come up in conversation or I'd see something on TV that would take me back to that day and rekindle the burning question of what it was that I heard. The only person that I had ever shared this experience with was my mother. She was quite open to the possibility of ghosts and psychic ability, and we often had in-depth conversations about the meaning of life, why we are here, and a host of other spiritual or religious topics. Unfortunately, during all of our conversations, neither of us could answer, with any certainty, if what I experienced was real or not. So with that, I let it go and went on to other things, like girls! I was a teenage boy, after all! Friends became very important to me and I enjoyed spending time with them. At this point in my life, I was still not a big fan of school, but enjoyed going just to be with all of my friends.

A few years after I had heard the mysterious voice, but before I became a big shot sixteen-year-old with a license and a black Ford Mustang to drive to school, I was home from school with a sore throat. Since my mother worked and my brother and sister were in school, I was home alone doing my favorite thing, watching TV.

That day still stands out for me. It was a sunny fall day, sometime after lunch. I was lying on the couch watching TV and out of the blue, loud and clear, I heard, "Mark!"

Someone had called my name. Again! Startled doesn't even come close to describing my disposition as I jumped up from the couch and turned to see who had come into my house without even knocking on a locked front door. Whoever it was had a male voice and the sound, once again, came from right behind me. No one was there. *Holy crap, it happened again*, I thought!

Now shaking, I had no idea what was going on, but I now knew that what I had heard the first time was real. No loud lawn mower this time. As I took a deep breath and tried to calm down, I still wasn't sure what to think, but I was either going crazy or someone was trying to get my attention. But who? And why?

I sat there just listening and waiting, but nothing! Only the sound of the TV and outside traffic occasionally going by. Hearing a voice outside was one thing, but now it's in my house... or in my head! I went back to watching TV, though my mind was now somewhere else.

I kept going back to that first occurrence and all I could say to myself was, *I knew it!* Time, however, has a way of making life's events seem not so real as we try to recall them from memory and that was happening to me. Now... hearing my name called a second time... it brought that original experience right back to life and now I was determined to find out what was going on more than ever.

Where does a teenage boy start looking for answers when it comes to the paranormal? At the time, my Atari video game was the closest thing we had to computers back then. There was no Internet to access. We did not live near a public library and I wasn't driving yet, so I did the best I could. I looked for books dealing with metaphysical subjects, even from my school library. Of course, this wasn't really the best place to find quality material on the subject, believe me, I checked! What books I could find, I purchased when I came across them. It appeared my quest for answers was going to be a long one with a slow start. My interest in finding answers, however, never waned.

One goal to get me started was to find a credible psychic to speak with, someone who may be able to bring me the answers I was looking for. Growing up in a small town limited the places that I could look and no one knew of anybody who was psychic, or should I say, anyone who was brave enough to admit they were psychic. There certainly were no metaphysical shops or psychic fairs where I lived. For the time being, I would just keep reading books and watching sporadic TV specials or documentaries dealing with the subject matter, whenever they came on.

As a senior in high school, I was fully committed to being a volunteer fireman and running with an ambulance as a certified EMT. School continued to be a great place to hang out with friends, but I loved being an emergency responder. Fighting fires, even as a junior fireman for a short time, was quite exhilarating and a possible career choice that I was looking into for the not so distant future.

When I finally graduated from high school, I fell right into a position as a 911 dispatcher after a friend who knew of an opening suggested I apply. It was a part-time position to start, which was perfect for me considering I just started college. For the next four years, my goal was to study hard at college while working as a dispatcher and continuing to volunteer as a firefighter/EMT. It was a great time in my life! I'm proud to say that I graduated with a 3.49 GPA.

An interesting spin on college for me was that I thought I could take a little psychological look at myself by majoring in psychology while working my way into parapsychology, however, the university that I attended had nothing even close to that subject and the ones that did were just too far away from the life I was loving at that moment.

One thing I wanted to check out while studying psychology was psychological disorders which caused people to hear voices. What I learned about that was, sometimes people hear voices. Even their names called. *Oh crap, I'm nuts*, I thought! But wait… there seemed to be a few other elements missing from my quick diagnosis to count me in as nuts just yet.

I found out there are varying degrees of crazy, so this didn't help clarify my mental status or the issue of what I had experienced. Maybe I was nuts, maybe I heard a voice from a higher place, or maybe I should just call it a day and head to a college party with my friends. Yep, party wins this time! Quest postponed until a later date.

It didn't take long and I was right back to my search. At one point, while still in college, I became very excited about the launch of a TV show that captured my interest immediately, *Sightings*. It was a show that dealt with all the topics that I loved—ghosts, UFOs, psychic mediums, spontaneous human combustion, and more. It was my favorite TV show at the time and I couldn't wait for the upcoming week's new episode to air. It reassured me that there was more to life than what we think we know and many more things that we just don't understand.

The possibility that I had experienced something supernatural was now more of a reality. It had to be real! The people on TV are the experts and they say it's real, right? After all, they are on TV. HOWEVER, the question still remained. What did I experience when I heard my name called? Although I completely bought in to the fact that hauntings and other supernatural abilities could be possible, something kept me asking if I truly believed it was real. Even though I wanted to believe that what I heard was supernatural and I wanted ghosts and psychics to be legitimate phenomena, I still couldn't bring myself to commit to the notion wholeheartedly. Again, for a time, my quest for real-life answers would have to wait for a more practical time in my life.

Shortly after graduation and now working as a full-time 911 dispatcher, I was sick at home and in bed with a severe case of strep throat. While sleeping, I was awakened later that night by the fire department pager going off reporting a car accident around 12:30am. With the shape I was in, I hit the silence button and tried to go back to sleep. After about 15 minutes of failing to fall asleep, I became panicked for some reason and something told me to get out of bed and go to that car accident.

As bad as I felt, I dragged myself out of bed and responded to the scene. Upon my arrival, well behind first responding EMS personnel, and as I walking towards a car that I could plainly see had gone down over a bank and head on into a tree, I was grabbed by my brother, who was also a fireman, and pulled away from the accident. It was then that my brother told me that my best friend, Scott, was in the car and was killed.

Worst experience of my life up to that point! I took two unusual things away from this experience that I always held on to throughout my life. I remember the overwhelming panic and pull for me to go to the scene when I otherwise would have never gone, feeling the way I did that night, lying sick in bed. But something or someone told me to go, marking yet another strange occurrence in my life to look into later. The second thing I took away was a very strong connection to my friend that seemed to persist even after his death. I don't know how to describe it other than it felt like he was still with me at times. He would even appear very vividly in my dreams. Scott would later be my inspiration and strength to join and persist through a very rigorous State Police basic training academy and I dedicated my career to him. Thank you, buddy!

It's weird, but I just sort of fell into the State Police career, as well. Much like the 911 job, a friend already working with the State Police suggested I take the State Police test when there were position openings. I did, passed, and made it through. I'd have to say that my inquisitive mind, skeptical personality, and love of excitement were a perfect fit for this job. Not to brag, but

I excelled at most of the units I was assigned to within the department. If you find a job you love, chances are, you'll do well at it. I can't recommend that enough. I started out like every Trooper, as a uniformed patrol officer. I then had the opportunity to transfer into a vice/ narcotics unit, where I remained for ten years. I could fill a book with stories from that position! Finally, I became a criminal investigator working major crimes. I can be a bit of an overachiever when I'm doing something I love and I have done my job well. However, in the beginning, just starting out with a stable career, being a first-time homeowner and finally out on my own, I now had the time and the means to re-establish the search for my answers. What did I hear? Who could have called my name? And what's up with the whole getting pulled out of bed, Scott thing?

So off we go…

Chapter 2
MTV Rocks

Jump ahead to life in my mid-20s. Up to now, I have spent a lot of nights reading books on hauntings, psychic mediums, and the basic principles of metaphysics. Cool stuff, but I'm no hard core believer yet. I have, however, grown tired of just reading about the subject and was looking for some more concrete evidence of the supernatural.

I thought the most accessible, and probably the easiest to find in the quantity I needed to make some reasonable observations, would be to locate psychics, mediums, or psychic mediums. For those who are not familiar with the difference, a psychic has the ability to gather psychic impressions about people, places or objects and predict future events or past occurrences. Mediums can talk with the dead. Not all psychics are mediums but most mediums are psychic. So, not being psychic myself, I had no idea where to start looking.

The commercial boardwalk was one option, but I just couldn't bring myself to trust a psychic in a tiny booth at the beach for some reason. I figured they were more for entertainment and, in my mind, if a medium was as good as they should be, they wouldn't have to work on the boardwalk and would have a large client base just from word of mouth. At least by now, people were much more open to psychic mediums and they could be found if you looked hard enough. So that was my goal and intended jump off point for my long awaited venture into the obscure.

The yellow pages seemed the most logical place to find a psychic, but not one was listed—no surprise there. Next, I thought I'd try the word of mouth thing and ask around for referrals to a good medium. Strike two! Ok, what next? I was out of ideas, so I just kept my eyes open and checked out a lot of public bulletin boards at libraries, restaurants, and so forth, in hopes that something would be posted somewhere. They say what you focus on becomes your reality. The law of attraction states that if you focus on something long enough, the Universe will help it manifest into your life. I found that may be true!

I used to be a big fan of MTV, back when they used to play music videos. However, when I was in my twenties, I had already given up watching that network for some time. This may have been my very first sign that I was getting "older." I'm not sure when or why it happened, but how could I give up watching MTV? Anyway, I did, and it had been a few years since I had last tuned in.

One day, I'm watching TV and scanning through the channels when I came across something that caught my attention. What it was, I don't remember, but whatever it was, I stopped and watched just as the program was going into a commercial. What happened next had to be more than coincidence. After spending the last few weeks totally focused on trying to find a medium somewhere within my reach, the very first commercial that came on a national network that I had not watched in a very long time, was a commercial for a metaphysical bookstore right in my backyard. The store has long since closed, but the name at the time it was in operation even struck a chord with me—"Possibilities Bookstore."

I was certainly looking for possibilities and being just a few minutes away, I knew I was going there. I found the timing very interesting because, as I mentioned earlier, I was a big fan of TV. I've watched hour after hour of TV and, just when I started looking for a medium, up pops a possible lead as to where I may find one, on a channel that I never watch, but had just decided to check out at the exact moment the program was going into a commercial. THE commercial! Was it a sign? Maybe.

Fifteen hours later, I was in my car and headed to the bookstore. The closer I got, the more excited I became, and when I finally pulled up in front of the business, BAM! A "Sorry, we're closed!"sign was highlighting the front door. The fun meter just hit zero. Since I made the drive and was already there, I figured I'd be nosey and go peek through the windows to see what this store was all about. Much to my chagrin, when I got to the front door, there hanging just below the taunting closed sign was a poster for "private, professional psychic readings" with a woman that I will refer to as Sue.

Holy crap, now that was a sign! Figuratively and literally! The Universe seemed to have led me right to what I was looking for—the first professional psychic medium that I could meet in real life. MTV, you rock! I copied the phone number that I was required to call and leave a message to make an appointment, and as soon as I got home, my fingers were dialing.

As the phone connected to the number and the ring tone was ringing out, I heard a click and got excited in anticipation of hearing the answering machine message. Yeah pathetic, I know, but I had looked for someone to talk with for a long time. To my surprise, instead of hearing the recorded message, the sweetest English accented voice answered the phone and, in a very polite and comforting tone, a woman introduced herself as Sue. A bit taken aback, I stuttered and introduced myself and explained that I was anticipating the answering machine to kick on and was not expecting someone to pick up. Sue laughed and said that she usually does not pick up, but was just going through her messages, so she did. This lead to a wonderful thirty minute phone conversation, an opportunity that I later learned not too many people had the privilege of experiencing.

From the first phone call, I knew that we had a great connection and would be friends. Sue filled me in on how her readings worked and set up a time and date to come and meet with her at the bookstore. This would be my official beginning as a paranormal investigator.

After waiting several weeks for my appointment to come, the night was finally here. I felt that since Sue was booked up for several weeks before I could even get in to see her, it was probably a good sign that she had some level of competency as a medium and people liked her. My goal was to test her, while objectively looking at what she had to tell me. The question was, how was I going to test her? This was my first experience with a psychic, and I was not really versed on how to test them outside of a few university studies that I had read about, but she would certainly have known what I was up to if I employed those methods.

Looking back on what I learned about mediums from books, I realized most people seemed to go to them to connect with family, friends, and loved ones. I thought I would take a different approach. I had read a little about spirit guides and thought this may be the way to go. Spirit guides are essentially people who have lived a life, passed on, and are now assigned to guide the living through issues in their lives. Some spirit guides are with us for our whole life, while others come and go to help with particular needs when they arise. My plan was to see if Sue could give me a reading that only dealt with spirit guides, since she would be expecting me to want to connect with family.

For the two weeks leading up to my visit with Sue, I spoke out loud to my guides, saying, "Guides, if you are really with me and can hear me, I want only you to come through during my reading." That felt a little weird at first, as I was talking out loud in an empty room to, well, I didn't know who, but after a few times of doing it, I felt like maybe there was a collective group of people on the other side that I was talking to in my imagination and the weirdness went away. My intent was put out, my expectations clear, but now, sitting in front of Sue, the only thing on my mind was, *I Can't wait to see where this goes.*

We met in a small conference room where people came to participate in a variety of metaphysical events and lectures. There were two chairs sitting in the middle of the room facing each other with about three feet of space between. I guess I was expecting a much smaller room, lights low with some candles or something. In reality, I felt more like we were right out in the open, sitting in the middle of a pretty big room with nothing around us except Sue's appointment book on the floor next to a very big bottle of water. I had a tape recorder with me, that Sue suggested I bring along, and a notebook to take notes. My initial thoughts on what I felt the experience was going to be like were a little off. It was a little less spiritually dressed, I guess. But what did I know? I had to stay objective and stop anticipating.

Sue invited me to sit down and asked if I had any questions. I had a million, but kept them all to myself. Sue began to explain how she works and told me that she will get information from spirit (whoever that may be) and it could relate to me personally, including such things as my health, career, finances, matters of love, or it could be connected to someone I know. Sue began by telling me that she was being told that I needed to be careful about how I handle my money. She told me that she was being shown some issues with a check register and that it was causing tension at home. Sue was off to a great start! I had literally just had a "discussion" with my wife because I had a very bad habit of living off of my ATM card, but failing to record the debits in our mutual checking account register. Amazing! I was apparently being called out on it by spirit, but who? Who the heck told her about that issue?

Continuing on with the reading, Sue then said, "I have a spirit guide here for you."

Wow, just what I asked for! Sue gave me a formal introduction to this guide. She told me who he was and why he was with me, and for the next forty-five minutes my reading was all about spirit guides and information from spirit guides. I was blown away, to say the least. So much so, that at the conclusion of the reading, I asked Sue if this was a typical reading. Sue stated that she usually hears from deceased family members, but for me, it was all about spirit guides for some reason.

Did I say WOW already? Not only did I get exactly what I had asked for, served with a side of "not a typical reading," but there was this amazing possibility that I had spirit guides, that they heard me over the past two weeks, and they came through during the reading, just liked I asked. What an awesome experience for me. I should also add that the information that Sue received from spirit for me was spot on, too.

Either she was talking to someone who was with me for a while or she was able to pull things from my mind. Or both! So many possibilities now entered my thoughts. So many different ways I could go with this, but one thing was for sure, Sue had my attention.

Instantly, I asked for another appointment and Sue recommended that I schedule the next session at least three months from the first one in order to digest what I was given and as not to become a psychic addict. Apparently she could tell I wanted more of this in a big way. A lot more!

After years of working with mediums and visiting different psychics, I have seen how people become addicted and dependent on psychics and rely on them to make life decisions for them, rather than living their own lives. Sue told me about this early on and I have witnessed it firsthand many times.

One thing that I have learned by observing people who are being read by psychics is that psychics do not like to make your decisions for you. They will offer information and possibilities however it is up to the individual to make their own life decisions. For me, my interest in visiting psychics as much as possible was to see what, and how much, was possible of spirit and the medium, more so than getting personal information for myself.

With time, Sue figured out that I was testing her in different ways. It was done in a very respectful and fun way and she was perfectly okay with that. With her acceptance and encouragement to test her in any way I wanted to during my readings, the road for observing and learning was wide open.

Let the fun begin!

Chapter 3
The Matrix

The more time I spent with Sue, the more questions I had. By this time, I had grown to trust her impressions. The information Sue received was far beyond generalizations or reading body language, or any language, since I barely said a word. For the most part, I just sat there quietly as the information poured out of Sue's mouth. I'd give an occasional head nod in agreement with what she was saying, but otherwise, Sue spoke and I took notes. There were also times when I just couldn't relate to some of the information Sue was giving, but in time, most of it had been revealed to me. That which did not make sense, Sue would tell me to put on a shelf for now and see what came of it later.

As our sessions progressed over a period of about two years, a routine was established between the two of us. I would arrive and engage in some small talk about life. Sue would say we need to get started because she had other clients coming straight after me. We would sit down and she would ask her expected question, "Do you have any questions before we get started?" and I would give my typical response "I do, but I'm not going to tell you." We would both laugh because it became an almost habitual question and answer session for us, but Sue innocently asked each time. There were predetermined questions that I was interested in having answered and nine times out of ten Sue would hit them without me asking first, which was the point of not asking the questions beforehand. I wanted to see how often she could cover my questions without me bringing up the topic.

During one session with Sue, she suggested that I try and would benefit from a form of Japanese energy healing known as Reiki. Along with helping the body heal itself, it was a way to increase a more positive flow of energy into the body and raise a person's consciousness or vibrational frequency. Being the inquisitive person I am, I thought it was worth checking out. Sue was a Master Reiki Practitioner and teacher of Reiki, and I was so impressed with the accuracy of her information that I had no reason to doubt her when she told me it would help. Not to mention, it was something new I could test.

Sue administered the Reiki and gave psychic impressions while I lay on a massage type of table. I was given instructions before we started that I may feel energy, see colors, hear buzzing, or a few other physical sensations. I didn't experience anything other than Sue's very warm hands as they hovered about three inches above me. When she was done, I was impressed with the psychic reading, as usual, but left feeling kind of neutral on the Reiki. I was much more relaxed than normal, but didn't have any of the reported sensations that many people report and was disappointed. But I agreed to try it a few more times. Sue also suggested, because of the stress load of my work that I begin meditation. I found that tempting, as she explained all the physical benefits from meditating, along with quieting the mind and raising one's consciousness even more.

Over the next several months, I had a few more sessions with Sue wherein I received both Reiki and a reading, and had been meditating for a few months now. For the most part, my meditations were uneventful. The idea was to quiet the mind and boy did I get pretty good at that by zoning-out for a good hour, but not so far that I would fall asleep. Time got away from me on occasion, as I would "re-emerge" and notice that what felt like just minutes was actually an hour or more.

That wasn't an easy thing to do with a wife and kids but they were kind enough to leave me at it. I settled into a routine of meditating almost on a nightly basis anywhere from ten minutes to an hour. Then, on a very quiet night in a very relaxed state, I had something happen. With my mind as silent as could be and my body in total relaxation, I had a spontaneous flash of an image in my mind. It actually caught my attention because, if you have ever meditated before and remember thoughts popping into your head and then catching yourself and quieting your mind again, it was nothing like that. It was noticeably different. It actually felt different. It sounds weird, but I could feel it in my head as I saw it, and it was fast! I do remember very vividly though, seeing a tall black woman in a beautiful long, purple dress that appeared to be of African descent based on her clothing style. She had long hair, a beautiful smile, and was standing at the top of a stoop in front of a red brick apartment building in a city "feeling" location.

I remember saying to myself, *What the heck was that?* It was so different from anything I had experienced before while meditating. I wrote it down in my notebook so I wouldn't forget the details and planned on making that a key question the next time I met with Sue which, luckily, was in about two weeks.

Even though I was not quite sure what happened, I kept asking myself if it could have been a spirit guide. Maybe that's how they introduce themselves, I thought. I had read a lot of material about spirit guides, but experiencing them is different, so I wasn't sure if that could be what happened to me or not.

Over the next two weeks, I meditated every night in hopes of a reoccurring experience to back up what I had seen before my next meeting with Sue. Unfortunately, it did not happen again. Of course, I planned on sharing with Sue what I had seen, but I began mixing up the face of the woman I had seen in my meditation with a woman called the "Oracle," a character in a 1999 science fiction action thriller film called *The Matrix*. It was one of my favorite movies that I've seen at least a dozen times before. I was getting frustrated because I was losing the image of the woman in my memory and replacing her face with that of the Oracle from the movie. The weird part was, they didn't even look remotely similar to each other or appear to be close in age, as the Oracle was much older. Whatever the case, this was my BIG question for my next visit with Sue.

At last, the night of my appointment with Sue finally arrived and I was filled with wild anticipation. I could not wait to ask if she knew what I had experienced or if it was real, and maybe even confirm that it was a spirit guide. This was the first time I had butterflies in my stomach going into a session since my first meeting with her. I wanted very badly some type of confirmation and validation that I was able to break through the barrier and have an experience like so many other people I have read about, even though it lasted only about a second. As I walked closer to the door, I took a deep breath and tried to hide any anticipation that Sue might pick up on and went inside.

We talked for a few minutes, sat down and Sue asked me her usual, "Any questions before we start?"

Hell yeah! I heard in my head, but went instead with a casual demeanor, "I do, but want to see if you get them first."

Being very familiar with my response, Sue started the reading. Blah blah blah blah blah, I think was all I heard for the first few minutes because I have a very hard time being patient when I want something and I was not hearing anything remotely close to what my only question was this time. But then it struck!

"Did you have communication with spirit recently?" Sue asked.

I didn't know what to say as I welled up with excitement. My heart was beating really fast and all I could say was that I wasn't sure and that was going to be one of my questions. Crap! I just broke one of my rules and gave too much info. I never should have said that was going to be one of my questions, but it was already out there.

Sue continued, "I'm being told that you have had communication, and..."

She stopped. *Don't do this to me,* I thought. Sue? Come on! The pause was killing me.

Sue started laughing and nodding her head, as she was apparently listening to spirit, but she wasn't saying anything. Sue then turned to me and said, "I'm being told that you have had spirit contact recently, but I'm not sure how to explain this to you. Have you ever seen the movie *The Matrix*?" Sue asked.

My jaw hit the floor and I started laughing, almost in tears, I was so blown away and totally speechless. I composed myself and told Sue that I think I know where this was going and that I did, indeed see *The Matrix*, many times.

Sue explained that I had a spirit guide with me. What I experienced was this guide introducing herself to me in a way I would understand, but my logical mind was getting her confused with the Oracle in *The Matrix*. This guide told me that it was okay and I didn't need to worry about it. My subconscious mind was making me see her as the Oracle to give meaning to what I saw as a spirit guide, rather than a random black woman standing in front of a building. It was apparently how my mind was trying to give me the association that she was a guide.

Done! I was completely done! My brain was fried. I did not even tell my wife Lauren what I had experienced in that meditation because I really wasn't even sure what it was that happened. Sue knew all of it and apparently from the disclosure of this beautiful spirit. Sue was able to pass along additional information from my guide and told me that anytime I wanted to call on her for guidance, just call her name and she would be there for me. Sue gave me her name, but that part I am keeping for myself.

In the years to come, I have called on my guide many times. I never saw her again like I did during that one amazing encounter in my mind, and as much as I wanted to, even in meditation, I could not get her to appear like she did. A long time after, I had the chance to ask Sue why I could not get her back like I saw her the first time. Sue told me that she received impressions from this guide that I just needed to see her once to let me know that she was real and around me, and all I needed to do was call on her from then on. It was not important to see her again.

My time working with Sue was some of the most unanticipated spiritual growth that I have gone through, including learning Reiki from her. My goal when I started though, was not about my own personal spiritual growth, but to see if psychics could accurately provide personal information, predict the future, read the past, and of course, tell me what I heard when I was younger. This one could do almost of all of that, but what she couldn't do, was answer my question about what I experienced when I was twelve? She just couldn't get any information on it, but told me it sure sounded like it could be a spirit guide.

Through the course of many sessions, Sue showed me that some people can possess a great amount of psychic ability. However, I wondered if they were all the same or if they had different levels of ability? Are mediums born with the ability to talk with the dead or can people develop that skill at any point in their life? And, what about ghosts? Sue was very good at what she did, but she seemed to connect with higher level spirits, angels, and deceased people who would appear to be in a place that we would call Heaven, or at least somewhere other than here on Earth with us. I still had a lot of questions that remained and a ton of new ones! My goal now was turning more towards hauntings and finding out if ghosts were real, rather than endlessly looking at new ways to see what Sue could do. She more than proved herself to me. I hoped looking at hauntings would also complement what I have learned about mediums.

I had seen a flier for a local paranormal research group hanging on the bulletin board of the same store where I met with Sue for the past two years. It listed their meeting time and dates and stated they were looking for new members. During one of my last few visits with Sue, I had asked her what she thought about paranormal teams and she gave me a firm and resounding, "I don't like them!"

Ouch, I thought! Sue followed up with some thoughts that she found them to be very disrespectful to spirit and told me that spirits were not toys to be played with. That's all she had to say about that. Being that I had just recently had a great spiritual experience of my own, I thought I better play it safe and let the idea of jumping into a paranormal team go for right now. The last thing I wanted to do was offend the spirits I had just connected with and Sue was very concrete with her words.

I guess change is inevitable and sometimes, what seems like a bad thing at first can really turn out to be a good thing later on in life and open up more possibilities that we were not aware of before. The news came that the bookstore was closing and Sue was moving her work out of the area. We kept in touch by phone for some time after, but as life grew busier for both of us, we lost touch with each other. Just as I learned that spirit guides come and go throughout our lives, apparently being assigned to us based on our specific needs at that time, and hopefully teaching us what we need to know while we're together, people are often very much the same. I will always have fond memories of my time spent with Sue and will honor all that she taught me.

Chapter 4

Dawn of the
Ghosts Hunters

After losing contact with Sue and over the next couple of years, I continued to seek out local psychic mediums, became interested in a show on TV called *Crossing Over with John Edward*, where John would connect families with deceased loved ones, and continued to experiment with the Reiki energy work that I had learned from Sue.

When dealing with mediums, I had found that there were indeed, a great variety of shapes and sizes. Each has their own unique way of working, receiving information, passing that information along to people, and dealing with their client's responses. Some psychics seemed spot on and others were way off, or just not connecting the information for me properly. There are varying degrees of psychic development for people and much of the authenticity or validity for me came with the presentation of the information by the psychic.

For example, if you have to ask questions such as, "Who is George?" or "Do you know someone with an 'A' name?" Chances are that I probably do know someone whose name begins with the letter "A" or a George somewhere out there, just like every other person alive.

On the other hand, if you tell me George is my cousin who died at age twenty-seven in a head-on car accident with a cow and wants me to tell his sister, Debbie, to stop bringing up the way he died—now that would grab my attention more so than asking who George is. This is just an example, of course. I don't actually have a cousin George and I'm sure Debbie's brother and the cow are both fine.

As much as I liked finding and checking out psychic mediums, I was still being pulled toward hauntings. That ever-burning question was still in the back of my head. Are ghosts real? After spending so much time studying psychology, I was even more uncertain. Is it possible, based on what people think about hauntings, that they can actually create "ghosts" in their mind instead of having ghosts actually present in a physically and completely independent conscious form of some type, in a building or home? It doesn't stop at homes or businesses either. What about cemeteries, battlefields, and other historic locations where many people all report seeing the same ghosts at different times? Can something influence the mind to make different people all see the same thing? Maybe all the new ghost hunting shows popping up on TV can help me answer that question... or so I hoped.

Most paranormal enthusiast will remember when a new show aired on the SciFi Channel (now called SyFy) in October of 2004 called, *Ghost Hunters.* Much like when the show *Sightings* aired in the 90s, I was really excited and hoped that this show could provide me with the answers about hauntings that I was looking for.

The show seemed legitimate and the promos indicated it was going to be a reality-based TV show, so I was hopeful it was going to be as insightful as it appeared. For the first time, a paranormal team was being videotaped doing complete investigations of haunted houses for TV. When the premier finally aired, I thought it was the coolest show going. Not only did the investigators take a more technical approach to investigating hauntings but they were also trying to debunk the activity to see if there were any normal causes that people were just misinterpreting. The team also presented evidence from time to time—very cool stuff and I was immediately hooked on the show. Because of my spiritual reservations, at first, about joining a paranormal investigation team, this was the next best thing for me.

It wasn't long before a variety of other paranormal TV shows started popping up. There seemed to be a dawn of a whole new generation of TV shows dealing with the supernatural that took off like never before. The shows that came after Ghost Hunters did not capture my attention like I thought they would, which surprised me. I enjoyed watching many of them for comparison of their investigating styles, but there were times when I wasn't really thrilled with what I saw. There were other paranormal shows that I flat out just didn't like.

By watching, however, I did learn that there were a variety of beliefs among different groups with many ways to approach hauntings but no common standards of investigating to follow. I found that the content of these shows dealt more with teams investigating the hauntings and collecting evidence, rather than trying to stop the activity for the clients. This only added more questions to my already full mind. Can hauntings be stopped? How do you stop them? Why is a particular location haunted anyway? Why on Earth would a spirit stick around at a place like a battlefield after they died if there was a heaven to go to?

As much as I loved watching these shows and couldn't wait to see what the next episode brought, I was still left feeling a bit empty. TV wasn't providing me with the answers I needed and now I had even more questions than before. I certainly was more open to the idea that ghosts exist and I was definitely more hooked on the idea that, at some point, I wanted to start investigating these occurrences for myself.

I asked some of my friends to check out the paranormal shows and give me their feedback about the shows and hauntings in general. As I mentioned earlier, back when I first became interested in the paranormal, it was not talked about much and most people would not admit they had a haunting, saw a ghost, or had psychic abilities. You'd have to be crazy to say something like that.

By the time the shows had been airing for a few years, people were becoming more open about hauntings and began to share some interesting stories with me. If nothing else, one thing I can say about the TV shows dealing with the paranormal genre is, TV really brought the topic of ghosts to the forefront of broadcasting and people were much more comfortable coming out of the "haunted" closet and talking about their experiences. People were starting to feel less crazy and more like they were not alone. One thing that I have consistently done in my work with the paranormal is to let people know that others are going through similar experiences and that they are not alone. That in itself has helped families feel better.

On the negative side, pun intended, many of the investigators featured in some of these shows engaged in what has become known in the field as "provoking." Essentially, investigators would do or say something to make a spirit angry in hopes of causing a physical response of some sort, such as something being thrown, a door slamming, an audible voice, or whatever it is that could happen. I couldn't get past the idea that, for the most part, the investigators had no idea who was haunting each location, why the ghosts were there, or what the intent was behind any of the physical activity that was taking place. I know that if there was a chance my grandmother, aunt, or anyone else I knew was there, I wouldn't want a group of strangers coming in and treating them so disrespectfully, and in some cases, being just downright mean. Most likely the ghost has been there a long time and considers that space theirs.

I understand that the big goal of ghost hunting is to try and document activity but many groups are limited by this and don't have, or choose not to have, metaphysical resources to try and identify who is there. Many teams just want to conduct "scientific" based investigations, but to what end does provoking help? It may result in physical activity but the clients already assume their place is haunted; otherwise the investigators would not be there.

Provoking can't help identify a ghost and it certainly does not help stop the activity. In some cases, just the opposite occurs, investigators engage in provoking, stir up the spirits, document what they can, and leave for the night. The problem is they have left some rather upset spirits there to now take it out on the clients. The same clients they were there to help.

These techniques make no sense to me. I would agree that there are some cases that provoking may be necessary and beneficial, but only when there is a plan of action in place to resolve the issue. You don't see that on TV too often.

All in all, I have to say, TV has done more good than harm with bringing the paranormal to light. More people are now calling for help when they would never have dared to in the past for fear of being made fun of or called crazy. Twenty years ago, you could not jump on the Internet and browse through the hundreds of paranormal teams in each state like you can now. Most people didn't even know where to start looking for help and they suffered for years in fear of the unknown.

Paranormal teams continue to start up around the country and that is largely because of the paranormal TV shows. My only wish now is that producers would start showing some of the more beautiful and amazing stories behind some hauntings, instead of making everything seem scary and evil. From what I have been told, most spirits stay here because of a traumatic event, emotional or psychological issue, or in fear that they will be damned to hell because of something they did in their lifetime. Better to stay here than take a chance of going to hell, right? But TV doesn't portray ghosts as people who often get themselves in a bad situation and need our help, or help from the other side. They don't explain that being able to experience a haunting is witnessing life after death first hand. How amazing would that be? It is only scary because we are told it is scary. It can be startling when you're not expecting to see a ghost, and there can be some bad spirits in the mix, I'm sure, but I'd bet more times than not, if ghosts do exist, people are just experiencing someone else's life in another form. People need to see it for what it really is. And, it is what it is, no more, no less!

For me, television networks airing such a wide variety of paranormal shows ended up being the straw that broke the camel's back. Although the content of each program being aired and the evidence that was being presented was compelling, it only gave me more questions than answers. As much as I wanted to believe what I was seeing, I couldn't. I don't know why, maybe because TV shows are entertainment based. I had to know for myself and I knew at that point that the only way I was going to be able to find out if ghosts were real was to physically insert myself into those places where people were reporting the hauntings.

And so it began...

Chapter 5
Enough Messing Around

It's funny how the universe works. Several years ago when I was looking to find a psychic medium, like a beautifully prepared meal served on a silver platter, I was hand served everything I asked for. Looking back at my childhood, I received most of the things that I wanted, and it seems that was no coincidence either. Perhaps there was something to this law of attraction concept that people seem to be talking about these days. As a young boy, later a teenager, and even as a young man, when there was something I wanted, I would almost obsessively think about what it was that I wanted.

If you ask my wife, she will most likely confirm that I'm obsessive. The funny part was, at some point down the road, I almost always received what I was obsessing about. Something would always happen to make it possible. There were times when it was really fast and other times when things seemed to unfold slowly, over a few years, but as things fell into place, what it was I was looking for seemed to become available. There was still some hard and persistent work involved on occasion but it seemed like the Universe was listening.

Lying in bed one night watching an interesting program on TV that had something to do with hauntings, it finally struck me—I had enough! Right there, lying in bed, I decided I was done watching TV to find my answers. Done relying on celebrity ghost hunters to tell me what was real. Done worrying about what was spiritually right and wrong based on what other people were telling me. I turned to Lauren and said, "Enough messing around, I'm going to do this myself!" I had hit my limit on relying on other people to find my answers.

When you break it down to its simplest form, a haunting is a very spiritual matter. How a haunting is perceived is largely based on a person's religious beliefs and teachings mixed with cultural ideals and public opinion on the subject matter. What I am trying to say is, just like finding your way to your own personal truth when it comes to believing in God, whatever God you believe in, if any, or trusting that there is an afterlife, wherever that may be, believing in ghosts is the same thing. You have to find your own truth for what is real or what is just perceived. Someone else cannot tell you something is so and make it real for you. So, I was going to find out for myself. After all, I investigate! That's what I do. Being a criminal investigator, I had done thousands of investigations. I knew how to look for things. The question was, what exactly was I looking for?

After my direct and unexpectedly determined announcement to Lauren, she looked at me and much to my surprise; she told me that if I was going to do this, she wanted to as well. And so it was decided, the two of us were heading into uncharted personal territory to explore the world of the haunted. You may have heard the expression, "Up the creek without a paddle." We didn't even have a boat! We had great intentions, but now that we had made this colossal decision to investigate the weird world of the paranormal, we didn't exactly know how to get started. It didn't look that hard. We logged hours of viewing ghost hunting shows. They all seemed to have similar core elements that we could work from. But after talking about it, what we came to realize was that what you can't learn from TV are the things you don't see on TV. Most of the shows were only half-hour episodes, so what happened during all the off air time that we didn't see?

I knew a little about investigative styles used for technical investigation and I had years of book knowledge and practice testing psychic mediums, but I didn't know much about the esoteric half of paranormal investigating that was largely ignored by TV and had concerns about negative entities or energies dwelling at a haunted site. Nobody told me how to deal with it. Lauren and I decided we were going to look for an already established team to join and hopefully get some hands on field training. It seemed like the most logical place to start.

For a few days, I made several futile attempts to locate the paranormal research team that had posted their flier on the bulletin board at Possibilities Book Store a few years ago. No matter where I looked, I just couldn't seem to track them down.

A few days later, Lauren and I were having a conversation with her dad, Richard or "Rich" as most people called him. Rich also had a great interest in the paranormal and loved watching the same shows we did. He informed us that there was a man that he worked with who belonged to a local paranormal team.

Wow, I thought, that's convenient! Rich told us that he would talk to him and see if they were accepting new members. A few days later, at our next visit with the in-laws, Rich had a name and number for us to call and a website from his co-worker for us to check out. We did and were really quite impressed with the information we found on that webpage. I guess I was expecting grave stones and skeletons but the website was put together pretty well and leaned more towards the scientific side of investigating paranormal events rather than hokey imagery. I liked it, Lauren agreed, and the site had a contact form to complete if someone wanted to become an investigator. We filled out the form and a few days later, we were contacted by the Director and invited to join their next meeting.

When meeting night finally came, I plugged the address into my GPS and we were on our way. A quality that every paranormal investigator should have is to be open minded and remain objective until you have all the information needed to make an educated opinion.

As we arrived at our destination, we pulled up to this very tall, dark, gothic looking church that sat upon a bit of a hill. From my initial impressions, I thought we were getting ourselves into something that was going to be a little weird and had expected seeing members with black fingernails wearing black lipstick and eye shadow. Maybe I'm exaggerating a bit, but I had some thoughts on who we were meeting. They did tell me their house was a church, but I didn't know anyone who had actually lived in an old church before.

When we went inside and met the two team Directors, who also were the homeowners, they certainly were not Gothic at all. In fact, they seemed very intelligent and friendly. We were introduced to the rest of team and inducted into the group. It was a great mix of people and we could tell instantly that, for the most part, they were skeptical, yet open minded about the paranormal. Their goal was to debunk as much as possible and see what was left. The team was looking for hard-core evidence and I guess I was too.

Lauren and I received some training from the team and were versed on their policies before we were allowed to attend any live investigations. The time came when we were finally able to attend our first investigation and I was really excited and a little hesitant about what to expect. It was to be a two-story house where the likes of a ghost had been scaring the client's two young children. I had thoughts rushing through my head as we drove closer. What would I do if I actually saw a ghost? Would it try to interact with me? Did the team have some weird initiation ritual that I needed to worry about having sprung on me? Did the home have a clean bathroom? The latter is a whole other obsessive issue I won't go into! Let's just say I like really clean bathrooms and leave it at that.

We walked through the home with the client as they told us their stories of ghostly encounters, which I must admit, did give me chills. The clients completed their tour with us and departed for the night. The home was ours now and the investigation was underway. We started with setup of the equipment. On edge, I kept a close watch behind me. Even with the lights on, I was anticipating something to jump out from somewhere. Setup was complete and we were divided into teams. Six members occupied the house and two teams investigated while the other two investigators sat at the "command" area and monitored the closed circuit TV cameras we had set up.

Throughout the night, my mind flashed through different possibilities of what the clients were experiencing. We did our best to debunk some things, but at the conclusion of the night, we really didn't have any more answers than before we came. What did I experience during this highly anticipated first investigation? Nothing! It was quiet. Very quiet! The home to me felt very comfortable after I got over the initial concerns I had. I have to admit, I was quite disappointed as we drove away that night and had a head full of different questions on the way home. The Director discussed the possibility of finding evidence on audio or video as we went through our recordings, but I wanted to see the historically sighted "woman in white" walk down the hallway. Where was she? Not here, apparently!

The most important thing that I learned from my very first investigation, that still holds true today for every single investigation that I have been a part of, is that you can never, ever anticipate what is going to happen on an investigation or expect things to go a certain way. Anticipation and expectation are two surefire ways to bias your mind and lead you away from being objective. It doesn't matter if you expect to find evidence to prove a haunting or anticipate a building will have no activity. Your mind will help you achieve either goal if that is what you are already thinking. This holds true even after the physical investigation. You never know what the evidence review will produce and your mindset can make the difference between catching something good or dismissing every sound you hear.

This is one aspect of criminal investigating that carried over to my paranormal research. It is very important, even more so for criminal work, to realize that you can never believe what someone tells you on face value and you must use you own impartial judgment, only after looking at all the facts, or you may make a very bad decision in the end.

The idea of remaining objective definitely proved to be the right move for me during my first investigation analysis. After several hours of reviewing audio of a very quiet second floor bedroom, a weird sound appeared on the recorder. It was very fast and had I not remained objective, I may have stuck with my initial thoughts when I left the house, that nothing was going on, and dismissed the sound as just random noise. I rewound the audio to listen a second time and discovered there was someone speaking that sounded like a little boy. What was significant about the voice I was hearing was that the clients were reporting a young child being in the house. I listened to the recording in amazement several times and was convinced this was a little boy's voice.

Amazed as I was, it was the only piece of evidence we captured that night. It was hardly enough for me to determine that a haunting was taking place, and certainly not enough to say it was coming from a ghost. I would admit however, that it was something of a paranormal nature, but what? I was not sure yet. Staying objective and keeping an open mind is the very first thing I now teach new investigators, in both my role as a criminal investigator and as a paranormal investigator.

Lauren and I continued working with this paranormal team for a while, learning the ins and outs of investigating, why to use specific equipment and when, how to objectively look at potential evidence and a whole lot more. For the most part, our experience working with this team was great, but as time went on, we grew more and more confident that we would be leaving the group. It was an extremely difficult decision to make, but one thing that we both felt was lacking, and probably the most important job paranormal investigators could do for a client asking for help, was to be able to bring resolution to the haunting, to stop the activity, even if I personally wasn't seeing any myself. It was clear that we needed to leave the group and develop our own resources in order to achieve this goal.

By the time we had made this decision, I had already run a few investigations for the team, developed a reporting system to utilize on cases, and dealt with clients before and after the investigations. I had a pretty clear idea of what I needed to do to run a case. My time working in a Vice/Narcotics Unit offered me plenty of experience being in charge of multi-agency, multi-jurisdictional investigations wherein I had to coordinate large scale operations at times. Running one small paranormal investigation at a single location with only a handful of people was a piece of cake in comparison, but there was a lot more to our decision to leave than that. During the two year period I spent with this team, there was growing interest from several co-workers at my full time job to get involved with our exploration of the supernatural. I had made several failed attempts to get them to join the team we were already a part of, but after persistent pressure from them to start my own team, coupled with my growing thoughts on becoming a resolution based investigator, and throw in a tarot card reading advising us to do so (more on that later), the time had come. Lauren and I left the group! It seemed the Universe again, had lined something up for me and it was already there waiting for us.

Chapter 6

It's in the Cards

About the same time that Lauren and I were contemplating starting our own group, I learned about a very well respected psychic-tarot card reader named Tara who lived about forty-five minutes from our house. Being that I had never worked with anyone who read tarot cards, I thought she would be someone very interesting to meet and I was curious as to what kind of information could be provided through the use of tarot cards. I had no intention on testing her and made an appointment for a general reading. Since Lauren was very interested as well, the first session with Tara was to be with Lauren. In the end, this may have proved to be more validating for me than I originally knew because I was not physically present at the reading but some of the information Tara provided was directly linked to me.

Tara gave a very accurate reading to Lauren. Much of the information Tara gathered was through the use of the tarot cards, but she also received psychic impressions as well.

Near the end of the reading, Tara asked Lauren if she had any questions. Lauren told her that we were members of a paranormal team, but thinking of developing our own group. With no other information provided by Lauren, Tara shuffled her cards and laid them out in front of her. Tara began to give very specific information about the current team we were with and Lauren was able to confirm all of it.

This certainly helped make the forthcoming information more trustworthy. Tara told Lauren that she strongly felt we should start our own team and that there was a house waiting for us. Kind of a weird statement I thought as Lauren was describing her session to me.

Tara continued and told Lauren that there was a woman with an "A" name, possibly an "Alicia" who had a home with a lot of paranormal activity and the home was waiting for us to come. Kind of creepy, actually! Tara told Lauren that, even if we didn't leave our current group, we should not bring them to this investigation. Tara said this would be the jump off point for us and we needed to do it on our own. Tara then asked if we had met the woman with the "A" name yet. What Tara didn't know was, we had!

As word about my involvement with a paranormal team started to spread around the rather large station where I worked, I was approached by a woman whom I had known for a very long time. She worked in our administrative department doing clerical work and her name was, get this—Alicia!

Alicia told me about her family homestead. It was un-occupied at the time, but the home was fully furnished and family members would stay there occasionally. Alicia described the homestead as often being referred to as a mansion back in the day, around the time it was built.

Not exactly a mansion by today's standards, but for this area it was a very large house. It was a two-story home with two staircases and many bedrooms, dated back to the late 1700s to early 1800s, and the owner was associated with the local railroad that used to run through the area. The home was in the small community of Suscon, Pennsylvania.

For anyone who has never heard of Suscon, it is a very unique, three-mile long town of consolidated weirdness. If something strange were to be experienced, Suscon was the place to experience it. For decades, unusual reports were made including, UFO and bigfoot sightings, murders, suicides, plane crashes, death by drowning, odd lights in the woods, cars that roll uphill, numerous fatal car accidents, black powder mill explosions, witches, Wiccans, devil worship, and ghost stories galore. This town had it all, and the homestead Alicia was telling me about was no exception.

Alicia explained that generations of her family have reported seeing ghostly figures and something resembling a large, menacing black dog or demon type of animal figure. For the most part however, what the family believed was there were just their ancestors. They were not afraid, but wanted to make sure there was nothing harmful residing in the home and that their ancestors were all okay. Now knowing that there were people out there who looked into this type of activity, Alicia told me that her family was interested in having the homestead checked out. Where else but at a very old and very creepy looking homestead in one of the most bizarre areas I have ever heard of, would Lauren and I be initiated into doing our very first investigation with a brand new team of fairly inexperienced investigators, if we were to do it at all? So, did we leave our current team and actually go for it? You bet we did!

Up until now, almost every significant change in my life, and every opportunity I have ever had to progress to something more, has fallen into my lap. My dispatcher job, my State Police career, finding my first psychic, joining my first paranormal team, and now having a phenomenal group of people ready to start a new team all seem to have been placed before me at absolutely the right time. To me, it seemed to be part of some strange, grand plan from the Universe to set me on an unknown path to something else. I know that sounds crazy, but this lady just told Lauren a house was waiting for us, and it was! All of it was crazy!

It took quite a few weeks and many conversations between Lauren and I, and the folks I worked with, but Lauren and I finally came to the conclusion that we had the right group of people with the right intentions at just the right time. The stars had somehow aligned and we would start a new team. It would be known as The Pennsylvania Paranormal Association, or The PPA, for short.

The new team members were excited, to say the least. They all had a great interest in investigating, but wanted to be a part of a smaller, more in-depth type of team, making The PPA a perfect fit. Lauren's dad, who had provided us with the information about the first team, also joined us, along with two other members of our former team who were looking to get more involved. So with that, our team was comprised of nine members in all—a realtor/insurance agent, three State Police Criminal Investigators, two federal investigators from the FBI, a public safety officer from a local college, a municipal police officer, and a satellite engineer. All credible people and all trusted with a very large amount of responsibility in their respective full-time careers. Almost all the members were involved in public service type of careers as well, which I liked. They were already helping people in various ways. Not too shabby of a start!

Our main goal was to put together as many resources as we could to identify the possibility of a haunting, or rule one out, and to then bring some kind of resolution to the clients concerns. Even if some of our members didn't personally believe in ghosts, we wanted resources who did and who were willing to help our clients. The way we saw it, if the clients were right and really needed help, what would it hurt to let someone like a psychic medium help them and, at the same time, it would give us a chance to study mediums at work in a live situation. Everyone was on board.

I personally still wasn't sure where I stood on whether ghosts were real or not, though it didn't affect our decision to create a resolution team. I had already talked to enough clients in the past couple of years who were asking for help and seemed to be sincere in their requests. That was enough for me and I thought it was important to try and get them help if they really needed it, and from someone who had the ability to help.

The nice part about this team was that, we designed it to be comprehensive in the way we approached each situation. A comprehensive investigative approach! We wanted as many angles to look at the reported activity as possible, in order to figure out what was going on at a site. We purposely put skeptics on the team to balance out the members who were hard-core believers. I've found that skeptics often come up with the very best reasons for why things happen. That then gives us something to look at and test.

I designed a principle that would guide us through our investigations. It was the principle of "A Realistic Alternative Explanation." What that meant was, if we could find an alternative explanation for the reported or witnessed activity that was occurring, and it had a realistic explanation that we were able to easily reproduce, we could dismiss the claims of being paranormal and go with the probability that we had the most likely cause of the activity by the alternative explanation, and label it normal. If we did find some legitimate type of paranormal activity, our goal was then to try and separate the normal from the paranormal. We wouldn't be doing anybody any favors if we let them think every occurrence on their property that seemed out of place had a paranormal cause to it, but more on that later. For now, let's just say that it was time to get to the house that was waiting for us.

Chapter 7

Things That Go Bump in the Night

A team should be trained, and trained well before conducting any type of serious investigation. Lucky for us, we already had several guys with years of electronic surveillance training from the world of undercover drug investigations. They were proficient in audio surveillance for criminal investigations, and investigating the paranormal was not much different. A few tweaks here and there, some minor protocol adjustments and we were all set on audio training. We were fairly well versed in video recording, as well. Now, getting to know the rest of the equipment was a different story.

There is a lot of equipment used for many different types of testing and monitoring during investigations. A large number of factors can influence the equipment, and investigators have to know what will normally cause meters to react or detectors to activate. Our group was familiar with a lot of the gear already, but we spent a considerable amount of time playing with each device to see what would cause reactions and what would not.

After we trained ourselves silly, got a very good grasp on what our gear would or wouldn't do in a normal environment and knew exactly how we were going to use it, we were more than ready to tackle our first big case—the "homestead" of Suscon.

We heard the claims, we prepared the team, and we knew the crime, but who was the perpetrator? Metaphorically speaking, of course. The family had experienced many encounters with spirits over the years and wanted confirmation of who may be there and why, or if there was anything harmful on the property. Our van was packed and off we went.

Pulling up to the homestead at dusk was a very unique experience. I had been on a variety of investigations, before The PPA was formed, but most were fairly average looking places. We investigated many occupied homes, a tavern, and a police station, to name a few. The homestead was the first that looked like a truly haunted house right out of a horror movie.

Surrounded by overgrown flower gardens and knee-high grass, the homestead sat off the main road, back about 100 feet, with a large front yard. It was dark and ominous looking on the outside because of its aged condition. The home had a wraparound porch, still lined with old porch furniture, and one couldn't help but to visualize people of old moving around the property and enjoying time on the front porch overlooking the gardens. Large overgrown trees and bushes now surrounded the home and it gave me an uneasy feeling as we approached, almost like someone was staring at you from the second story windows. The house had many windows, so no matter where you were outside, you couldn't escape the feeling that someone was watching you.

We had pulled into an old gravel driveway and parked. As I entered the driveway, I couldn't help but think of a story one of the family members had told me before coming. Years ago, when the family lived in the home, the mother would gather the kids and walk to the end of the driveway together each night. This was a normal routine when the sun went down, just before the father returned home from work. It was told to me that the mother was afraid to leave the kids in the home, but the person who told me this was not really sure why. The home was always known to have paranormal activity, even back then, and the family presumed this was the reason why they all left the house together to greet the father when he came home.

The view behind the house was of a very dark wooded area that grew even darker after the sun went down. The sound of a small stream trickling past the homestead could faintly be heard somewhere off in the woods. I had to keep reminding myself and the team to remain objective and not to anticipate anything.

The family met us outside in the yard upon our arrival. They certainly were brighter than the gloomy abode we were about to enter, wonderfully lively people with so many stories of sightings that we were starting to get behind on our schedule. As I've mentioned, it was just at the start of dusk when we arrived and we wanted to take advantage of whatever light was left for our set-up. The family gave us a quick tour of the interior of the home and departed for the night, giving our team of five investigators free run of the building.

When we first entered the house, the biggest thing that struck me, almost instantly, was the overwhelming amount of Christian artifacts. Religious pictures and statues, crosses and rosaries covered every room in the house. I found the scariest picture of Jesus that I have ever seen in my life and was later told that it came from a European country and was very old. Either someone in the family was very religious or something was going on there, or both! Whatever the case, the inside was no less creepy than the outside. I believe, in its day, this was an amazingly beautiful home. All the furniture from generations past was still present and most of it was in very good condition—a bit dusty though, I must admit.

After about an hour inside, I still had that horror movie feeling inside me, but tried to remain as objective as I could. This was no easy task with Mother Mary and Jesus looking at me from every angle. Nonetheless, we had a job to do and it was time to get to work.

We established our command area outside of the main portion of the home. I assigned the investigators to two groups, one team of two and a second team of three. One team would monitor the security cameras and the second team would actively investigate their assigned areas of the home.

Falling back on my criminal investigation experience, we kept a running log and strict report of all investigator activities and their locations throughout the entire investigation. It was very important to know exactly where each person was at all times. Each team was also assigned a camcorder, which always had to be recording from the time they left the controlled command area until they returned. This acted as a log of events to visually show us where each team was at any given moment, and also as a control device to reference, should we need to compare any audio later for anomalous sounds or help rule out investigator contamination on other recording devices. All the equipment was set up, the audio reorders were running, and we began the physical investigation.

Within minutes of beginning the investigation, three of our members had some unusual activity on the second floor in one of the bedrooms. In an area that was previously checked, with no indicators for EMF, otherwise known as Electro-Magnetic Fields, the team now seemed to be getting strong EMF spikes in that area. There is a common belief among paranormal investigators that EMF spikes can accompany the presence of a spirit.

Tim, one of the investigators present, suddenly became extremely fatigued, while Jen, a second investigator, witnessed some form of dark shadow move from the ceiling area, down a wall, and disappear. The EMF readings remained for a few more minutes and then stopped as suddenly as they appeared. The team removed themselves to the command area to discuss the events and also to give Tim some time to gain his strength back after becoming weak. This was the first time that Tim, and the rest of the team, experienced someone becoming so fatigued during an investigation.

I had read that mediums can become fatigued while working with spirits and the theory was that a spirit can somehow drain their energy to create physical manifestations. We had to keep this in mind while trying to understand what was going on and make sure Tim was okay.

Throughout the night, investigators continued to have experiences, some subtle, such as hearing strange sounds and knockings, and others a little more profound, such as an event I witnessed. As I sat in the living room on the first floor with Chris, another of our investigators, I was keeping close watch on a Blessed Mother statue on a living room table. All of a sudden, a red laser line appeared in the middle of the room, approximately two feet wide, right in front of us. It lasted only about two seconds and then it was gone.

A piece of equipment that I grew fond of using on investigations was a Black and Decker laser level that I used for home projects. It was one of the first laser levels produced. My thought was that if a ghost can pass by a window with backlighting and block out the light, like so many people report seeing, it should have enough mass to block out a laser line. When you put a laser generator on one side of the room, with the laser line showing on a wall on the opposite side of the room, it gives an area of space for something to travel between and, hopefully, the video camera will pick it up and record it as it passes through the line. In this case, I set up the laser in the dining room and pointed it into the living room. Disappointingly, the camera did not pick up anything moving through the line and the line was not blocked out, but we certainly saw something reflect the light from the laser directly in front of us. What it was, still to this day, I do not know.

At the conclusion of the investigation, we were left with a bunch of personal experiences which were worth a better look. The bumps and bangs that were heard throughout the night gave us the impression that something unusual was going on in that home. It felt to everyone like there were more people in the house than just the investigators, and I don't mean the living. We still had to conduct the review of nearly 40 hours of combined recorded audio and video to see if anything may have been captured that would back up the client's claims of activity and our own experiences.

All of the data was reviewed over the next ten days. What we found was far beyond what we had anticipated, including four very solid EVPs.

EVP stands for Electronic Voice Phenomena and, in its basic form, is a voice that appears on an audio recorder which is not audible to the human ear at the time it is recorded. The unique thing about the voices we captured was that they seemed to be commenting on our conversations as we were speaking. Pretty creepy when you don't know someone's there with you! I spent hours trying to debunk the voices and looking for causes or contamination that could have led to the sounds appearing on the recorders, but the fact was they were there and I couldn't dismiss them.

What we had found seemed to back up the personal experiences that the team reported. Even Larry, our super skeptic from the FBI, was at a loss for the cause of the events we encountered that night. It was a great first investigation and the team did an outstanding job, taking a grounded look at all that happened, when it happened, and without faltering from their objective or getting spooked and running out of the house. We were all in agreement that something unusual was going on in that home.

The question remained though, what was going on? I was really excited about the discoveries we made that night and, for the first time during my two years of investigating, I finally had experienced something that I would consider paranormal.

Even though I had some strange things happen while investigating with our original group, no activity ever rose to a level that I would consider paranormal in nature. I couldn't have asked for anything more on the first case with my new team. It seemed that paranormal events could occur, but what was the cause?

It still wasn't quite enough for me to decide if ghosts were real. Unfortunately, I didn't see a ghost that night. I did see and hear a few things that were definitely not going on in any other home I had been in and we found some voices on our recorders and experienced things that I would definitely classify as "paranormal," but was it a ghost causing all the activity? It was hard for me to say. Could it have been some kind of weird energy or bending of time that briefly linked the past to show us a glimpse of what happened way back when? I can say that the possibilities were now wide open for me. I can also say that I was immediately addicted to what I had experienced and wanted to see more. I didn't see that coming, but if you remember back, I tend to have compulsive tendencies and I could easily see that there was definitely going to be much more investigating in my future. I was hooked, and determined to figure out what was going on, now more than ever. My poor wife, the things she would now have to put up with! It was time to ground myself and remember that I need to keep an open mind with no expectations, and lucky I did.

Chapter 8

The Ghost Effect

While The PPA was in its early stages, we began investigating homes without the use of a psychic medium. A medium that would meet our requirements was hard to come by. It was still my mission to put a resolution team together with as many resources as possible to help clients with a host of paranormal issues. Just like I had a difficult time finding reputable psychics in the beginning, it wasn't much easier finding credible mediums who would come out and work with a group for free. Since I wanted to study a medium at work in this environment, I didn't want money to be a motivating factor to get them to come out with us. Not to mention, I didn't want to pay someone to help other people if I was volunteering my own time. I hoped to find a medium who wanted to help people for the simple reason that they could.

Until the right person came along, we would do our best to try and identify what was going on in a home or business, whether normal or paranormal, and attempt to offer some type of relief in any way we were able.

One benefit of not having a medium working with us at first was that it gave me time to take a deeper look at the clients themselves. Just as I was trying to understand my experiences in the past by taking a look at subconscious possibilities, I was also looking at the client from a psychological perspective to see what they were thinking while describing the experiences they were reporting. I wanted to know not only what they were thinking, but also what they were feeling.

One question that kept popping up in my mind was, why do people perceive what they perceive when it comes to a haunting? While some witnesses report that they freak out and run when they see a ghost, others find it amazing or feel like the spirit is just part of their family.

The PPA receives a wide variety of different types of requests for help, and there seems to be just as many, or more, emotional reactions to ghosts and other paranormal activity as there are requests. So, I started to look at the people, along with the activity. Wow, did this open a whole new can of worms that, on a few occasions, I wished that I had not opened. Let's just say that some things are much better left in some people's minds and we'll leave it at that. However, there were some really amazing insights that came from this line of study that helped me understand that our team was on the right track with the way we wanted to evolve and investigate cases.

A common pattern was starting to emerge in clients with each new case we conducted. It's important to understand during an investigation what the client's reaction is when a paranormal event happens and the type of activity that they are reporting. Perception is everything in this line of work and it affects the way people report things to you, even if it is unknowingly wrong.

What I discovered was that there was something occurring with many of our clients. I call it, *The Ghost Effect.* I repeatedly observed that people will report having a real, or seemingly real, perception of an encounter with a ghost, or become an unexpected witness to a paranormal event, such as a cup sliding across a table. Then, after that experience, every odd incident becomes, "The ghost did it."

It doesn't matter if there are rational explanations for the incident or not. The person's mind has become instantly conditioned to believe a ghost caused the activity. From this point forward, many clients have a hard time staying objective and their mind can become their worst enemy, especially if they are scared. This is not to say that there isn't a haunting taking place or that some of the events that are happening aren't legitimately paranormal, but ALL of the events tend to get lumped into one big ball of HAUNTED, instead of being looked at individually.

One of my most memorable cases involving The Ghost Effect was in a very active home located in a small community in Northeastern Pennsylvania. The client had reported to us that the family was witnessing doors opening and closing and household items moving on their own. They were hearing footsteps throughout the home. Their pets appeared to become scared and run out of the room, or just stand and stare at something they couldn't see. The most disturbing claim was a black shadow figure moving in different areas of the house.

On one frightful evening, while the mom and dad were lying in bed watching TV, they both witnessed this black shadow figure peek through the doorway into their bedroom. They explained that the figure was featureless, but could make out a head and shoulders of what appeared to be a man that looked at them for about five or six seconds, then moved back out into the hall-way. Since they had no idea what they were dealing with or why this thing was in their home, they were worried about their children's safety, as most parents would be. Based on experiences like these, I can certainly see how people would constantly be on edge and have a hard time stopping their minds from dwelling on what was happening at night. I know I would be! I think in this case, it's understandable how the Ghost Effect applies.

We had visited this residence on two separate occasions to investigate. A short time after our first investigation, I received a call from the client. He was panicked and talking very fast. The client explained that, as he was sitting in his living room, a tiny candle-stick light lampshade from the chandelier hanging in the middle of the room popped off of the light bulb, flew through the air, and fell right on him. He freaked out, left the room and called me. This happened during the day when the activity was usually not as frequent. The client was not expecting anything to happen and this caught him off guard.

When we returned for our follow-up investigation, one of the first things we looked at was the chande-lier. It was designed with eight small candlestick lights surrounding the center. Each light had its own tiny lampshade. With just a quick examination, it was dis-covered that the tension rods that held the lampshade on the light bulb acted like a spring. In fact, I had a very hard time keeping the lampshades on the light bulbs because their natural tendency was to pop off. From an outsiders look at the situation, a "reasonable alternative explanation" had been found and it was easy to see how the event could have happened by natural means.

For someone who is chronically dealing with a haunting, their first impulse is to jump to the conclusion that "the ghost did it." However, a freight train travels past the house, about 50 feet away, twice every day. The vibrations from the train could easily rattle the house causing things to move around, and they did.

If you're curious about the findings on this investigation, I can say that this was another outstanding case for personal experiences and evidence. A few highlights that come to mind begin when Lauren and I were investigating in a first floor back room. Without warning, a very loud pop, much like a firecracker, rang out and scared the bejesus out of the two of us. A video camera monitoring this room showed absolutely no movement in the room, except us jumping three feet into the air, and we could not find the source.

A bit later, Lauren and I were sitting at command, watching the DVR monitor, and the client's digital camera that was hanging on a wall hook right next to us turned on by itself. This was certainly much more subtle than the loud pop, but interesting just the same. The client told us that had never happened before with the camera and, after contacting the manufacturer, they explained that it is designed not to do that and shouldn't have. Maybe someone wanted us to take their picture, who knows! Several EVP's were captured during the investigation, along with a few other minor events.

The highlight of the night came for Lauren when she was kneeling on the floor securing a camera cable and saw a man with a goatee walk into a doorway a few feet in front of her. When she looked up to say something, the man was gone. Lauren didn't pay much attention at first because she just thought it was Chris, one of our investigators, until he walked out of another room behind her. There was no way for him to get into the other room without going around Lauren and he verified that he had not been in the other room. Even more interesting, a prior owner of the property, who had passed away years ago, also had a goatee. Maybe it was him.

For Lauren, this was quite an amazing event. For me, just another experience reported by someone else that didn't completely solidify my questions personally, but it did give me a whole lot more faith that ghosts exist beyond what I've just heard about on TV. I now felt like I was on the right track!

Lauren was kind of a skeptic when it came to people's claims of ghosts, so for her to confess that she saw a man in the doorway that shouldn't have been there was a big deal. For the homeowner, we were able to bring him some insight in to what was going on, validate his experiences and give him our word that we would return as soon as we secured a metaphysical worker to help identify and remove whoever was there, if possible. We had used a few cleansing techniques before we left, and the client reported back to us weeks later that there was some relief from the activity. It was still present, just not as bad.

In cases like the one I just described, I've found that it is very important to look at each reported event individually. Every experience needs to be picked apart and the job of the investigator is to separate the normal from paranormal. If perceived paranormal events can be separated into these two categories, when the normal events happen again, the clients will then understand why and not become afraid that a ghost is there to harm them. The Ghost Effect is a type of post-traumatic stress from an extreme event or from continually witnessing paranormal events over time. Ruling out the paranormal from normal events and educating the witnesses are the first steps to helping them become grounded again. This affect can happen to investigators when they witness something profound during an investigation. If their

minds are left to run wild, investigators will be looking at everything as a paranormal occurrence thereafter,
rather than objectively analyzing it as a single event that
may have a normal cause. I will say it again; no expectations and no anticipation are a must! They feed the
mind. Our team has learned to pick apart every event
they experience.

There is an opposite side to The Ghost Effect when
investigators, or even skeptics, conclude that a place is
not haunted based on a very limited look at the location.
This is often an issue with new investigators and one
that I constantly have to reinforce to our new members
to avoid. It tends to occur in homes or businesses that do
not have a lot of square footage. The smaller the location,
the slower time seems to pass, especially if there is nothing going on, paranormally speaking. Quiet locations
are often the "nightmare" for investigators, much like
the haunting is for the clients. Putting it simply, at small,
quiet locations, there is less to check out. Investigators
are there to experience the activity the clients are reporting and then find the cause, normal or paranormal.
When nothing is occurring and everything that can be
looked into has been covered, investigators start getting
bored. I have heard investigators say, after being on a
case only two or three hours, "There's nothing going on
here."

My question to them is always, "How do you know"?
Is it fair to make a snap decision based on being at a
site for only a few hours on one night? When you break
down the most active places, generally there are only
one or two things that happen on any given day, and
most people will report that the activity isn't occurring
every day. Even with daily activity, if only one event happened on that particular day, you have to be in the right
place at the right time, looking in the right direction, to

experience that "one" thing. That's not an easy feat to accomplish. To be fair to the clients and to the location, more than a few hours should be spent investigating a site before any definite conclusions are made when no activity is present. Otherwise, you can really only say that there is no activity happening there at that moment, but not that a haunting isn't occurring. To say the location is not haunted would be presumptuous, unless you have been able to rule out, through the investigation, all of the reported activity as being normally caused. This is where I found that utilizing a credible medium can be invaluable.

Chapter 9

...And in Walks Biggy Gin

It has been said, "If you build it, they will come." Or so they said in the movie, *Field of Dreams*. That certainly seemed to hold true for me. Since the creation of The PPA, the cases have been coming in strong. Word of mouth seems to have been our best friend, and the unique mix of our team members may have appealed to people. Whatever it was, right from the start we have been at no loss for cases.

In the first year of investigating, we primarily worked on conducting very technical investigations. We were becoming proficient at documenting evidence and debunking many of the claims people were reporting. Our team was still operating without a medium and a few of our members liked it that way. There are teams that prefer to stay on the scientific side of research and don't want to deal with metaphysical techniques of gathering information, and by that I mean, using a psychic medium to investigate. I, on the other hand, looked at using a psychic medium as another opportunity to test their abilities in a setting where the metaphysical and the paranormal would overlap. The benefit to that would be, a medium can assist by providing historically significant names and events that may help verify claims of activity, normal or paranormal. Would a psychic medium come? My intention was out there. Would the Universe drop a medium at my feet again?

I have been a criminal investigator for a long time. When I look at a possible haunting, I am looking at a crime scene. There is evidence to be collected and a suspect to be searched for and identified. When the evidence points to the suspect, an "arrest" can be made. By arrest, in this case, I mean it to be the big moment when we can positively identify the ghost we are looking for based on the evidence that was discovered. The hard part, though, is finding the proof of the culprit's identity. Physical evidence can only get you so far. Unlike physical evidence collected at a real crime scene that links the suspect to the crime, physical evidence collected at a paranormal scene most often only provides proof that a crime was committed. In other words, proves a haunting is taking place. It won't necessarily tell you who the suspect is or why they are there. Many times, physical evidence may suggest or point to a particular person who stuck around in spirit form, but there still may be doubts about the spirit's identity and no solid proof.

That's where scientific based teams are limited when called in by clients looking for answers regarding what, or who, is in their home or business, and are looking to have the activity stopped. Scientific teams do, however, play a very valuable role in the paranormal community by studying the effects of a haunting on the environment and designing some awesome new equipment for investigators to better study and track the activity. I find the ingenious tools created by people in this field to be very helpful in my own work. I am very grateful for these creative inventors but, as a criminal investigator,

I want to go beyond the science and solve the puzzle of who is causing the paranormal activity and why.

As our team evolved, and a better understanding of what our clients wanted to get out of an investigation emerged, I contemplated the best way to identify a spirit's identity and reflected on all of our previous cases. I kept coming back to the same conclusion and, frankly, it was the same initial idea that I had from the beginning. The best chance for us to do the most comprehensive investigation possible was to bring in someone from the metaphysical community who understood the spirit world in a way that most scientific-based people would not. I believed, at this point, that I needed to step up my search for just the right person who was also willing to work for free.

I'm amazed at how the Universe works and of all the opportunities that have been placed before me and my team since we started. Out of the blue one morning, I received an email from a man named Chris B. Chris introduced himself only as a producer from a New York based production company and related that he had been going through our website and was interested in talking to me about a TV series that was under development. That was the entire email. Not very insightful, but definitely an attention grabber!

I responded with my contact info and shortly after Chris B. called me on the phone. I was presented with a more formal introduction and he explained to me that his company was developing a new show dealing with hauntings wherein animals seem to be largely targeted by the activity or somehow integrally involved in the haunting. Chris had found our website and was interested in a few cases that we had done which involved animals in one way or another. In particular, one investigation was of a large former insane asylum that later became an animal research facility followed by an electronics development business years later. The clients not only had a few encounters with something that appeared animal-like, but they also had a cat on site that appeared to be disturbed by the activity in various ways. Chris B. invited us to participate in the show if a network should pick it up.

Unique from most other paranormal shows was that the network would be using our team's footage from the investigation. Any filming by the network would come *after* the initial investigation was complete. I may have mentioned earlier that I have some obsessive tendencies and one of those tendencies was keeping strict protocols on how our cases are conducted. Lauren calls it being a "control freak," but I like to think it's being thorough. I'll take that title though, because running the most controlled investigation is what it is all about.

We limit the number of our own investigators on cases to reduce contamination and I knew I would really have a hard time trying to get my work done with a production crew following us around. We had accepted a few media requests in the past allowing local news crews to follow us through an investigation and I was ready to peel my face off before we were half way through the investigation.

It's a tough balance for me because it's nice to be recognized and get good information on the paranormal out to people via media outlets, but at the same time, I hate unnecessary contamination when I am recording for sound. We spend hours listening to audio recorders after cases and the last thing I wanted to waste my time on was backtracking a strange voice or sound for an hour and having it turn out to be someone who was with us. Unfortunately, the media and I have two separate, but understandable, agendas.

I have since learned how to incorporate the media into what we are doing and it's all good now. I called Chris B. back and told him to count us in. He advised that they were pitching the concept to a few networks that had some initial interest and would be back in touch with me if one of them signed-on the show.

We didn't hear back from Chris immediately, but all of a sudden, cases started coming in that seemed to have some type of animal connection. Honestly, it was just weird! Furthermore, right after speaking with Chris, I had a conversation with a woman, by chance, who told me that I needed to get in touch with a business owner named Linda. Linda owned a business in the Poconos area of Northeastern Pennsylvania appropriately called, the *Candle Shoppe of the Poconos*. According to this woman, the Candle Shoppe was having all sorts of strange activity, but most bizarre was that they thought monkeys haunted them. Yes, monkeys! It's actually not so strange after talking with Linda and hearing the background.

The building that now houses the Candle Shoppe used to be the home of a medical doctor. After the doctor could not save the life of his father, who died of yellow fever, he started doing research on spider moneys. Hundreds! The monkeys were secured in a cage in the basement and purposely infected with the same virus that killed his father, then their heads were cut off and the brain and spinal cords examined. Pretty gruesome for sure, but done in the name of science, if that makes it any better. If spider monkeys have any level of intelligence, they were able to see their fellow monkeys being beheaded and knew what was coming. The monkeys were then buried in the backyard of the house. But monkeys were not all that the Linda was reporting.

The employees believed there was a man lurking through the building and they had been told by two mediums not to go into the attic space because some-thing bad was up there. *Now this was a case worth checking out,* I thought! After all, who gets haunted by monkeys? Linda was so sure she had something going on in her business that she contacted the prior owner and asked about the cages in the basement and if anything odd ever happened when they owned the property.

The prior owner told Linda that they left the cages in the basement for the monkeys because they still ran around the building. Obviously, there were no living monkeys doing that. This is how Linda learned about the research lab that used to be there and about the mon-keys. Linda told us that she would normally have been surprised to hear something like this, but she felt, and heard, what sounded like a group of animals running past her and through the store, kicking up dust as they passed. The first time it happened, Linda fled the store and called her husband to come and lock up and has not since stayed in the shop after dark by herself.

I contacted Linda and introduced myself. I explained that I was given her name and number by a patron that had requested I call her because she knew the business was looking for some help. Linda invited our team to come and investigate in hopes that we could bring them some answers. We decided on a date when the store could be closed so we could have the whole building to ourselves.

During the time between our phone call and the in-vestigation, both Linda and I were going to do a little research on the property to see what we could find. We kept in touch over the next several weeks, sharing info, and Linda told me she was going to check out a near-by cemetery in search of the grave of the doctor who once owned the house. A few days later, Linda called me back and told me she was not able to find the doctor's gravestone. She told me that her sister had suggested calling a psychic medium, whom she had received several readings from, to help them locate the stone. The medium's name was VirginiaRose Centrillo. Linda related that her sister was so impressed with VirginiaRose that she thought it might be helpful to have her work the whole case with us. I thought that was a great idea. My only stipulation for Linda was that she was not to provide VirginiaRose with any information on the haunting or history of the business prior to her arrival, which would help keep her impressions legitimate and untainted by prior knowledge. Linda agreed and would set it up.

We conducted the investigation at the Candle Shoppe over the course of three visits. Virginia would not be joining us until the third. On the night of our first investigation, investigators had several personal experiences, including seeing a shadow move across a room on the third floor, having a window next to the investigators rattle aggressively for several seconds, feeling extreme cold spots, and having an investigator's foot stepped on by an unseen force. There was not enough evidence to positively document that a haunting was going on there, but definitely enough personal experiences to warrant a follow-up investigation. Several weeks later, we returned to the Candle Shoppe and conducted a second investigation. This time, we had absolutely no personal experiences, no physical activity, nothing! It was really quiet and rather disappointing. The more you do this kind of work, the more you learn that you can't expect or anticipate anything. You just never know what will happen, or in this case, not happen. So for now, we would have to settle on a quiet night and look ahead to round three, when we would finally be using a psychic medium for the first time.

Fast forward another few weeks and the night had finally arrived. It was to be a scaled down investigation with some handheld gear, only two investigators, and VirginiaRose, the medium. I was accompanied by Tim, one of The PPA investigators assigned to the prior two investigations at the Candle Shoppe. The store was still open and we had to wait until after closing to begin working, so we took a little walk around the property and hung around awaiting the arrival of VirginiaRose. I had never met Virginia before, but I did have the pleasure of speaking with her on the phone prior to the investigation. Linda had put us in touch to become acquainted. In the short amount of time we spoke on the phone, Virginia was able to provide me with all kinds of information about the location and what she felt might be going on there. So much information that I was a little concerned Linda had filled her in about the haunting. I later questioned Linda about this and she assured me that she had not uttered a word to Virginia about the activity or who she felt was there. You'll recall, when I first talked to Linda about Virginia coming, I requested that she not disclose anything about the activity or the location because I wanted to see how much info Virginia could give without us providing any insight. If you remember my sessions with Sue, that's how I work.

We were getting closer to investigation time. The store's customers had all left and Tim and I were hanging out and visiting with a few of the employees at the front counter when we heard a sudden commotion in the parking lot. It seemed to be getting louder and closer. All eyes turned to the front door and in walked Biggy Gin! It was VirginiaRose Centrillo and she was larger than life. Wearing a leopard pattern dress shirt, carrying a purse the size of a shopping bag, and sunglasses so big I could see myself in them from across the room.

Virginia shouted out a big, Queens, New York, accented hello to everyone and immediately introduced herself. This woman knew how to make an entrance and how to immediately command a room! I felt like she had just popped out of a cake and I was instantly fixated on her. She had a personality that made everyone comfortable with her right away and a crazy sense of humor that easily broke the ice. I couldn't wait to see where this night was going. Virginia brought two other people with her, her husband Chris and her friend Camille. Both have their own unique psychic abilities and often help her with her work. Virginia explained that she brought them along to help out and keep her company for the long ride home. It was a three for one deal! We now get to watch three very spiritual people work, and in their own unique ways. I was excited to get started. By now, you may be wondering why I call her Biggy Gin. That name developed over time and fit her New York mobster-gansta personality, which would appear unexpectedly from time to time when we were having some fun. After all, I did say she was animated. The Gin part comes from her having red hair. She's a ginger. She sometimes goes by that name, as well. You just never know who will come out when VirginiaRose is in town.

After introductions and some brief small talk, we were ready to get down to business. Since we never worked together before, I informed Virginia that we had already conducted a technical investigation and we were now ready to conduct a metaphysical one. I wanted to carry a few pieces of equipment with us as we worked our way through the three-story building and Virginia was fine with that. I told her that what I was looking for from her was to tell me what the clients were experiencing, where they were experiencing it, and what or who she though was causing the activity. I figured that should cover everything. Virginia laughed at me and said in a joking way, "Oh, is that all?" and graciously accepted the challenge. Virginia explained to me that her husband Chris would sit quietly in a corner and meditate. Chris had the ability to project his consciousness throughout the building and take a look at who was there in spirit form, and even talk with them. Virginia said Chris also acts as a battery for her by helping to increase the energy she works with in the building through his meditation. I wasn't quite sure if that was possible, but I was up for anything. Camille works just like Virginia and can see and hear spirit, or get impressions from the past. Virginia asked if Camille could work directly with us and I agreed.

As we began, standing near the checkout counter on the first floor, I provided Virginia with three options as a starting point, the first floor, the second floor staircase, or the basement door. Virginia started getting impressions immediately before we even moved. She told us that she was picking up a man on the second floor. She felt that he was a prior owner of the building and she was seeing medical equipment around him. Virginia then moved to the staircase and we followed her to the second floor. Camille began picking up impressions of a doctor, Virginia agreed, and we worked our way around the various rooms. Virginia provided us with a long historical list of impressions relating to the doctor and his daughter. She felt they both were still present on the property and that the doctor stayed behind after he died to continue his medical research. The daughter stayed to care for, what Virginia believed, were pet monkeys or perhaps even chimpanzees, and asked me if that was possible. I shrugged my shoulders, said maybe, and began following Virginia to the basement. As we were passing the entrance to the attic, Virginia stopped. She said she wasn't comfortable with the attic. This was the same area that the two mediums that patronized the store a year before had told the owner not to go into, and indicated there was something negative there. Virginia felt that this was an area where the doctor's daughter kept at least two chimps, but that there was also some bad energy in that space. We finished the second floor and it was time to move to the basement.

As we traversed the narrow wooden stairs into the basement, Virginia and Camille told me that they were both feeling ill. Virginia said she had strong emotions running through her of panic and fear, dread and death. Camille stated she was feeling the same thing. Virginia asked me if the employees were seeing shadows in the basement or some type of movement. I confirmed they were. Virginia stated she was hearing rustling and strange noises, but it was near the floor. Camille stated it felt like small animals. Virginia and Camille walked into the next room in the basement. The floor in this room was mostly dirt, but covered with wooden planks to walk on. It was poorly lit and cold, with stone walls that had been painted white. There were two distinct work stations and a very large screened in area in one corner of the room. Chicken wire walls created a large cage with a door that one could walk in and out. Virginia and Camille entered the chicken wire cage and Virginia stated that she wanted to throw up. Camille stated that she was overwhelmed with fear and death. Virginia told me that she felt little creatures there, like moneys grabbing onto her legs. I confirmed that there used to be monkeys held there. Camille said they were sick monkeys. I again confirmed the information. Virginia walked over to one side of the cage where a solid wall separated the cage from a work station on the other side. She noticed a small, round hole in the wall, about five inches in diameter, and said, "I wonder what this hole is for?" Virginia became quiet for a few seconds, becoming visibly upset, and exclaimed in a trembling voice, "Oh my God, this is where they cut the heads off the monkeys!" Virginia is a huge animal lover and seeing those images in her mind upset her so we removed ourselves from the basement for a time.

We all met back at the checkout area and woke Chris from his meditation. Chris related to us very similar information as what was provided by Virginia and Camille. When you add all the psychic impressions together from Virginia, Chris, and Camille, we had a very thorough idea of what may be going on in the Candle Shoppe. It seems that the doctor, who originally built the house, stuck around to try and finish the medical research he started. He killed hundreds of monkeys for his research and buried them in the backyard. The doctor had a daughter named Elizabeth who had pet chimpanzees. After she died, she felt she needed to stick around to keep them, and the rest of the tiny spider monkeys safe and protect them from her father. Elizabeth did not agree with her father killing all the animals, even in the name of science. Judging by the research that Linda and I had done regarding the Candle Shoppe, Virginia, Chris, and Camille seemed to be right.

Virginia wanted to do a cleansing of the building and try to release the doctor and his daughter. They were both trapped by their own emotional issues and, according to Virginia, weren't moving on like they should. We went back to the area where we found the doctor on the second floor. Virginia said he was still there, pacing back and forth. She said that she could see, in her mind's eye, that we were in what would have been the doctor's bedroom before the building was renovated. Virginia tried to have a conversation with the doctor, but he stated firmly to her that he did not have time for us and we needed to leave him be. I thought this to be a very strange comment considering we were standing in his bedroom. If I had a group of strangers show up in my bedroom all of a sudden, you bet that I would not be telling them that I did not have time for them and to leave me be. I asked Virginia why he would not be startled by our appearance in his bedroom and she stated it was because of the state of mind he was in. I remember having a few dreams that, after I woke up, I thought were absolutely insane, like driving a flying car for instance. While in the dream, I did not question why the car was flying, I was just flying it. After I woke up, I knew that cars couldn't fly, but it seemed real and logical while I was going through the dream. It appeared to me that the doctor seemed to be stuck in this same dream-like state and I questioned Virginia about that. She said, "That's it! Yes, that's a great way to look at it." This was the first solid answer for me to the question of why ghosts stick around and how they get trapped here in the physical world. Although there is so much more to it than that, and so many more reasons why they stay behind, but it was a start.

As it turned out, the doctor did not want to go. Virginia enlightened him on the fact that he was dead and told him how to look for the light when he was ready. The doctor felt he needed to finish what he started in his research and would move on in his own sweet time. She was able to help release Elizabeth and the poor little monkeys. After speaking with Linda, Virginia explained that the doctor wanted to stay and Elizabeth moved on, but would most likely come back to check in from time to time, and the monkeys were gone. Virginia also felt that there was such emotional trauma that had happened there, with all the monkeys being beheaded, that a residual haunting would still be present. What that meant was, people were still likely to see flashes of things that happened in the past as they replay in our present time. The sound of monkeys, or a sighting here and there, was certainly possible. We concluded the investigation for the evening, said our goodbyes and, I realized on my drive home, through a single phone call about a new TV series involving animals, a string of events occurred and the Universe had dropped another psychic medium at my feet. Biggy Gin told me that she felt we would be working with each other again in the future and that we would be back at the Candle Shoppe. Turns out, she was right!

Chapter 10

Lights, Camera, Action

It was almost a year since I last spoke to Chris B. from the production company. Our team was busier than ever and we had become extremely proficient at running investigations in a practical and very controlled manner. We limited ourselves to working on new cases, about two a month. This gave us ample time to review all the recordings we gathered, without rushing or diminishing the analysis, and still get back to our clients with our results and final recommendations within a two-week period. During that time, we had the fortune of meeting and working with a few very skilled psychic mediums. We utilized them as outside resources and divided our investigation into two parts, the physical investigation and the metaphysical investigation-resolution. We would conduct a full technical investigation with as few people as necessary and have a medium work on the site at a later time or date. We compared information from both portions of the investigation and looked for correlations between them, along with historical information that we gathered through our research.

On a few cases we had the medium on speakerphone while we were at the site investigating. As I mentioned earlier, there were a few people on our team that would rather have kept to conducting strictly technical based investigations, but we integrated the use of a psychic medium into our investigations rather seamlessly, so everyone was happy. The way we separated the technical from the metaphysical information, to objectively examine the psychic's ability, even appealed to the skeptics. It was a smart way to corroborate psychic impressions with historical facts and our investigation evidence. During this period in time, we had the advantage of observing a few different mediums at work in different ways. We were impressed with most of the feedback later reported by our clients, including a reduction in activity and a feeling of peace. Most of our clients were reporting significantly less activity, if any. Looking ahead to the future, narrowing the use of a psychic medium down to just one or two people that we could call on frequently seemed to be the most logical next step for our team and for consistency in evaluating them properly. Once we were certain that we had a credible medium to work with, we wanted to do a long term study to evaluate their methods of reducing activity to see if it actually made a difference at the sites we investigated.

Our team had come a long way since our initial investigation at the homestead. Cases were still coming in and our clients seemed to be happy with the work that the mediums were doing for us, but just when I thought things were going good, they got even better. Right after wrapping up a criminal investigation at my day job and heading back to headquarters with my partner behind the wheel, I received a phone call from a number I didn't recognize. I'm in the habit of screening my calls when I don't recognize the number, mostly because of telemarketers, but thought, *What the heck, I'm in the mood to see who is selling what today.* I answered the phone and, lo and behold, it was Chris B. from the production company. The show was sold and ready for production. Chris asked if we had any other interesting cases come in since he spoke with me last. Of course, my response was, "Hey Chris, do you like Monkeys?"

We were secured for two episodes of a brand new paranormal show to premier on Animal Planet in November of 2009 called, *The Haunted*. That was the most obvious network when it came to animal related shows, but the last place I would ever expect to find a paranormal show. Nevertheless, the topic was hot and all the networks were cashing in.

During the summer of 2009, we were scheduled to shoot our first episode. It was to be at the Candle Shoppe, where ghostly monkeys roamed the halls. We had worked with several psychic mediums by now and the producers had asked if we would mind them bringing one in for the shoot. They were aware that we had already worked with VirginiaRose at the Candle Shoppe, but the network had a few connections of their own they were considering. Virginia was our obvious choice, but they said it was in the hands of their executive producers and they'd let us know in a couple of weeks, before the start of shoot. While waiting for the day to come when we would be filming our first episode, I had a phone call with Chris B. to go over a few details from our investigation at the Candle Shoppe. Something Chris said reminded me about the case we did in Wapwallopen, Pennsylvania, with the flying light shades from the chandelier and the black mass peeking into the bedroom. What I didn't mention about that house was that it was connected to a Wiccan coven years ago, way before the owners moved in, and cats were stored in the home and reportedly sacrificed during rituals. One of the sounds that we recorded there was the sound of what can only be described as a tormented or suffering cat. The clients had no cats to make the sound, yet it appeared very clearly on our audio recorders. There were also rumors that a mix of occult practices had occurred there besides Wicca. After enlightening Chris on the case, we were booked for our third episode before we even started the first. By the time the day came to film the first, I had been given the nickname of "The Legend" by the producers because of the crazy types of cases that I brought to the production team in such a short period of time. They said I had a gift for finding great cases, but the only thing was, I wasn't finding the cases, they were finding us.

About a week before the start of the Candle Shoppe filming, we finally got word from the production company that, after interviewing several psychics, VirginiaRose would be the medium who would be working with us. We were very pleased to hear that. I thought it was only right, since she worked the case with us from the beginning and it was well deserved. She blew the doors off the place, as her information was so accurate. Apparently, the production team agreed AND, if you remember, Biggy Gin did say that we would be working together again in the future and going back to the Candle Shoppe. So, here we were! Again, everything seemed to have lined up and we were filming away. At the conclusion of the shoot, Virginia told Lauren and me that she really enjoyed working with our team and found us to be very professional. We felt the same about her. Virginia told us that if we ever needed her help, she was there for us and that we could call her anytime, day or night. Virginia had been doing this work professionally for over 30 years, so I found this compliment and offer very flattering.

We moved on to filming the other episodes for the show, and the production company brought a case to us from New Jersey that they wanted to film, but it had not been investigated yet. We agreed to investigate this new location, which involved a horse farm where horses, and other animals, were dying. The producers had called in another medium for that case named Barbara, who also did a very good job providing information. In the end, what we found through Barbara's impressions was that because the farm was a safe and loving place for animals, the Universe was delivering ill-fated horses there to die in the most compassionate and loving way possible. Now, there was no way on Earth I could possibly prove that, but we did find some paranormal activity occurring at the farm. Barbara provided accurate information to the family about their personal lives, and after what the Universe had seemingly lined up for me all along, who was I to question this? It seemed to make sense. If it were true, then the spirits present at the farm certainly were not bad, by any means, and this was one of the most beautiful hauntings that I would have ever been a part of. The funny part is, the family told us later on that they felt like they were there to take care of these animals in their last days, even though they did not know the horses would soon be gone.

We ended up filming two more episodes for season one of *The Haunted*, six in all for the first season, and it was a wrap for The PPA. The production company would spend the next several months filming a few more episodes with other teams that had also participated in the show and we needed to get back to our now growing backlog of cases.

Chapter 11

Things Aren't Always
What They Appear

Did you ever get the feeling that you were not alone? Many people in haunted locations have that feeling, but quite often don't know who or what they are dealing with. Unless the witness actually sees a very detailed figure in front of them, most just know that something isn't right and that someone else may be occupying the same space they are. Unfortunately, this is where rational thinking often ends and memory kicks in.

What most people know about ghosts is largely learned from TV or the movies. Hollywood has a way of sensationalizing pretty much everything to the extreme and ghosts are no exception. It's no fun going to a movie theater to watch a movie about a ghost doing the dishes or sitting in a chair watching out the window. Who wants to see a ghost just doing mundane daily activities? The way to get people to tune in to TV shows or go see a movie is to make it scary. Let's face it; sometimes it's fun to be scared! The downside to being bombarded with one horror movie after another or being exposed to television programming promoting the scary side of a haunting is that your mind is being programmed to believe that ghosts are there to harm you. There are some rare occasions where that could happen, but for most people, when first presented with a haunting in their home or business, they become frightened without even knowing who the ghost is or what it is all about. Why do some people immediately become scared? It's because their memory has been told that ghosts are scary.

When *The Haunted* finally aired on national TV, a funny thing happened to me over the following several months. I started receiving emails from viewers, and had also been told by several people that I knew who tuned in, that I was crazy for going into the places we investigated. They asked me if I was scared when I was there and told me that watching the episodes really freaked them out. I must admit, when I watched the episodes myself, I jokingly said to our group, "Those guys are nuts," meaning us, and "I wouldn't go into those places, they're scary!" The difference was, when we were actively investigating the haunted sites, we went through very long, quiet time periods with an occasional few seconds of excitement here and there.

Despite what you see on TV, paranormal investigations can be very long, and even boring, at times. But what aired on TV was nothing that I would call boring. It was a little creepy, in fact. During live investigations not yet edited for TV, there is no dramatic background music, no special lighting, and no startling visual effects to get the heart pumping. It's rather dry. It was very clear to me, at this point, that what was being aired on TV was programming people in a way that didn't truly reflect what was going on in a home quite the same way.

During a few conversations later on with the producers, they told me that this was the best way to try and recreate the emotional experiences that witnesses were experiencing. I suppose that is one way of looking at it, but it is strange to watch a scary version of the otherwise calm investigation that was conducted. For the team, it just wasn't scary when we were actually there. What an amazing transformation from investigation to broadcast, though. Watching the episodes on TV definitely elicited a different feeling in me than being at the location in person. What I realized going through the production process of a show was that even though the episodes are close to what really happened, they are still about entertaining the viewers. Some of the events were portrayed to be a little scarier than they actually were just by adding some special effects. My initial gut feeling was right when I felt that I needed to ignore what I was watching on TV years before and go find out for myself. Although real life investigations are similar to TV, there is a difference.

Shortly after wrapping up the filming of season one, Paulette, one of our investigators, was invited to a psychic party where a medium named Michele would be reading a small group of Paulette's friends. At the reading, Paulette received some pretty amazing insights from Michele upon speaking with her one on one. When Michele found out that Paulette worked with a paranormal team, Michele told her that she has been looking for a good team to join. Michele enjoyed working on resolving activity and paranormal teams had access to many of those types of cases where people were looking for resolution. It was very important to Michele that spirits were not left abandoned at a site after the investigation was over. If she could help them move on, she would like to be there to help. Paulette called Lauren and me a few days later and told us about her experiences with Michele and her interest in joining the group, so Lauren and I scheduled a date to meet her and receive a preliminary reading from her. Michele agreed to let us test her out and, if we felt she was credible, we would consider adding her to our team.

After finally meeting with Michele and receiving some very good psychic information, we told her that we would try her out on a live investigation and get feedback from the clients. If they were happy, we would include her as a member. This was a big step for us because, up until now, we had always kept mediums as outside resources. We had grown into a very busy group, however, and taking on all kinds of requests for help. We felt it would be beneficial to have someone as part of the group that we could call on at a moment's notice and who could dedicate their entire attention to helping out our team exclusively. In the end, this turned out to be the right decision. The learning experiences I was about to have may not have happened any other way.

It didn't take long before Michele proved herself in a big way. On her very first case, in fact! Much like we had asked Virginia at the Candle Shoppe to tell us what the clients were experiencing and where, along with whom she thought it could be, Michele seemed to have this ability, as well, and we received wonderful feedback from our clients at the conclusion of the resolution. After a few more cases, it was obvious that Michele could do what she claimed by reducing or eliminating activity in homes for clients. I personally was still searching for that ever-elusive sighting of a ghost, but by now, I was also growing into more of a believer that something I could call "paranormal" was going on. What that was, I still wasn't sure.

During the time that we worked with Michele, something was starting to stand out in the type of cases we were receiving. For some reason, people were starting to largely report sightings of black masses and what they thought were demons. When I asked why they thought what they were seeing could be a demon, the typical response was that it was a dark, featureless mass. Basically the same thing that the clients from the chandelier home reported, but they didn't call it a demon. I found this curious. Could it actually be a demon? I had a hard enough time believing a human spirit could be a ghost and now we're getting called for demons all of a sudden. And lots! The only way to find out, I guessed, was to go take a look. For some reason, the thought of coming across a demon didn't scare me. I guess I really didn't believe it was possible for them to hurt me and didn't put much stock in them appearing at your average haunting. When we were preparing for these types of cases, my thoughts were that we not tell the psychic and see what she comes up with. Although the clients were reporting a possible demon, the activity they were describing was still much like every other reported haunting and no more negative in nature. The claims in these cases were largely still very emotion-based, which led me to believe the clients were associating a black mass with something evil because of what their memory told them from movies or TV. Was I right? Time would tell.

I received a request for help from a woman who had recently moved into a brand new townhome with her husband and two teenage boys. It was located on beautiful country property where Pennsylvania farmland once occupied the landscape. It was the last place you would ever expect to find a haunting. During the initial interview with the client, she told me that when the family first moved in, they started noticing very subtle things, such as strange noises, knocks, and bangs. Over the next several months, the activity grew much more noticeable and was now starting to concern them a little. Unexplainable things would happen, such as the first floor bathroom doorknob jiggling and the door opening by itself. Strange and unpleasant smells would suddenly appear in the home and the sound of footsteps could be heard walking through the second floor hallway. The activity grew even more frightening when the boys' bedroom closet door began to rattle very aggressively and the sheets were pulled off the client and her husband while they lay in bed. The family was becoming afraid. The family cat would no longer go into the master bedroom, where much of the activity was taking place, and even if they carried the cat into the bedroom, he would run out hurriedly and not return. The activity rose to a level where the family witnessed a black mass in the hallway, but the final straw was when the client felt like she was touched and someone or something had tugged on her shirt. The client became frightened and started yelling at whoever was there that "this was their house and they had to leave." The client commanded that they "did not want them there" and to "get out." It was right after this physical contact that the client requested our help.

Being that the family living in this home was now scared to death and on the brink of leaving, we made this case a priority and responded as soon as we could. The team assigned consisted of three investigators and Michele, the medium. When we arrived, my initial impressions would not lead me to believe that a haunting was going on in this complex. The townhomes were beautiful and brand new, as I had mentioned. We had to keep in mind, however, that we needed to remain objective. Once we got into the heart of the investigation, we began having some experiences that reflected what the clients were reporting. Strange smells appeared from nowhere, odd sounds were heard and our K9, "Ben," whom we had taken on many cases, was alerting to the fact that someone was behind the bathroom door, the same door that would open by itself on the first floor. Many people believe that animals have a heightened sensitivity to energies that humans do not, and Ben seemed to be proving this. Because he was a specially trained police K9, Ben was perfect for use in the paranormal field. He was trained to work in unfamiliar locations and had many reactions for certain events as a police dog that we could convert for use on investigations.

Michele went to work right away and started picking up on the history of the property and much of the activity that was going on throughout the house. Michele felt that there was a greater amount of activity happening in the master bedroom than anywhere else. You didn't have to be psychic either to feel that the master bedroom was different. There was a very heavy feeling in that room as compared to the others. Once Michele had a handle on what activity seemed to be happening where, it was time for her to start tuning in on who might be there and her findings were very upsetting.

What the family originally thought was a demon in their home was actually a five- or six-year-old girl. The upsetting and sad part of this finding was that the little girl had drowned in a pond on the property many years ago. She was alone and latched on to the client because the client was a mom. The little girl was scared and desperately trying to get her attention. When the little girl grabbed on to the client's shirt, the client freaked out and started yelling at her. With the client now present and Michele relating this unfortunate information to her, the client broke down and started crying. The client told us, in a broken voice, that the little girl was reaching out for help and how must she have felt when she told her that they did not want her there and that she had to get out. It was one of the saddest and most emotional cases that I have ever worked on, to think what that little girl must have felt when she heard that "she was not wanted there" and to "get out" coming from the person she was reaching out to so desperately for help. The client, and most of my crew, was in tears as Michele helped this little girl go home. The happy ending to this story, however, was that after checking back with the clients, the activity had stopped, the girl was at peace and the family was no longer scared

Things aren't always what they appear to be in this line of work, and a great deal of what I have learned from this case was to take into account what the clients are reporting, but also keep in mind that there are a million other possibilities than what you originally think may be occurring. A little girl taught me that and it was one of my most memorable cases. What was originally thought to be something so negative that it was described as a demon was, in fact, someone reaching out for help the only way they knew how. Whether it involves someone getting scratched or pushed, or something being thrown at you, you still have to stay grounded and try to figure out what the underlying meaning was or what the intent behind the activity is before jumping to any conclusions.

Over the next several months, we didn't find any demons. What the clients reported to be evil or negative, for the most part, turned out to be nasty former homeowners, cranky family members, or just plain old rotten people causing grief for the new owners, just as a few examples, according to Michele. From my experience dealing with mediums is that what people most often mistake for an evil entity is often just a plain ordinary human spirit who was unhappy in life and remains unhappy in death. This comes from relying heavily on psychic impressions of the situation but, in most cases, those impressions were backed up with historical facts and really made perfect sense given the situation.

Michele helped a lot of clients along the way, as well as our team, and for that, I will always be grateful. Due to some increasing health issues, Michele wasn't able to continue working with us on investigations as we had hoped she could. She passed away a short time later. I'm willing to bet that Michele is probably still helping lost souls from the other side. Thank you Michele for all you have done for so many clients and for the compassion you showed for so many souls!

Chapter 12

Seeing Is Believing

A short time prior to Michele's passing, we had an emergency case that she was unable to make at the last minute. Remembering back to VirginiaRose's offer to help us any time we needed, I called her and asked if the offer still stood and that we were going to be heading out to the home the next evening. My hope was that Virginia would be available to be on speakerphone while we sat with the clients at their kitchen table. Since Virginia was living in New York, I wasn't about to ask her to jump in the car and drive several hours to meet us at the clients' home. Strangely enough, Virginia asked me what time I would like her to meet us there. I told Virginia that I couldn't impose and have her drive that far and a phone reading was just fine. Virginia again asked what time I wanted her to meet us there.

An amazing thing that I have learned by working with mediums for so long is that they can give very accurate readings on homes or people and they don't even have to be at that location. Virginia's persistence to work with us in person paid off, though! She wanted to come to the house, we needed help that night, and it ended up being the start of an incredible relationship that would move The PPA, and myself, to a much higher level.

I had asked Virginia to meet the team at a location just down the street from where we were going. Our team would often meet away from an investigation location prior to going in so that Lauren and I could brief the team on the case and our mission for the night. This worked out great because we could have Virginia meet us away from the client's home, as well, and we did not have to provide her with the location address. This helped maintain the purity of her information because she had no background information beforehand to work from. Once Virginia arrived and we spoke for a few minutes, Virginia bluntly told me, in a half joking way, that she has been waiting a long time for us to call her to come out so we could work together again, and she was very excited to be there with us. I told Virginia that I thought of calling her many times, since she had offered, but I just couldn't bring myself to impose on her by asking her to meet us so far away from where she lived. Virginia put me in my place and told me that, as the owner of a trucking company, she has made many trips to the West Coast by vehicle for business and a two- or three-hour ride for her was nothing. Virginia added that she loves to drive, loves to do this kind of work, and I better not wait so long to call the next time. My sincere apologies were offered and I assured her that, knowing what I now knew, I would not make that mistake again. The world was at peace between us and we were ready to take on everything else that was not. We had no idea what we were getting into.

Having had the pleasure of working a rather unique and complex investigation with Virginia already, I knew she wouldn't let me down the next time a really abnormal investigation came along. Not that any investigation is normal, but something definitely other than ordinary came along. I received an investigation request from a family who owned a three-story home just outside of Philadelphia, Pennsylvania. The claims of activity were some of the most physical and bizarre that I have come across with our team. The family was scared and wanted whatever was there out. I contacted the client and right away I could tell she was desperate for help. Although when I spoke with her on the phone she sounded completely sane, and I recognized that she was an intelligent woman, there was something that just kept giving me the feeling that there was a little bit of exaggeration involved with the claims of activity. There was simply too much physical activity being reported, or so I thought. Boy, was I wrong!

When it comes to poltergeist activity, seeing truly is believing! For those not familiar with poltergeist activity, it is, in part, as defined by Wikipedia, "A type of ghost or other supernatural being supposedly responsible for physical disturbances such as loud noises and objects moved around or destroyed. Most accounts of poltergeists describe movement or levitation of objects, such as furniture and cutlery, or noises such as knocking on doors." In all, I was in this home on three separate occasions and I can tell you from my personal experiences that the clients were definitely not exaggerating.

The family explained to me that they were witnessing extreme activity occurring over a period of three years, which now seemed to be escalating. A few of the events the family reported experiencing included coming downstairs in the morning to find the dining room chairs sitting on top of the dining room table, hearing footsteps throughout the house, coins being thrown all over, bedroom doors being blocked by items when no one was in a room, lights throughout the house turning on by themselves, children's toys being turned on, and items being thrown around in different rooms. On more than one occasion, items in the refrigerator had been emptied out onto the floor. The neighbors were seeing lights coming on and shadows moving inside the home when no one was there. The clients had actually seen a shadow figure in the home, and this was just some of the activity being reported. The most disturbing report that we had from the family, however, was that their infant had somehow moved from a crib in one room to a bed in another room. The baby could not even walk yet, let alone get herself out of a crib and onto a bed in a different room. This may give you some idea of why I thought there could be some exaggeration going on.

When we arrived on the night of the investigation, we found a very nicely decorated home. Very neat and clean. We had a game plan in place and, after meeting with the family and then setting up our audio and video monitoring equipment, we decided we were going to leave the house unoccupied while we went to dinner. The clients told us that, on many occasions, they would leave the house for a little while, only to come back and find things thrown around the house, or items stacked on top of each other, or items would be broken on the floor. When this activity first began, the family thought they had an intruder in the house, but the doors were still secured when they came home. After a few more experiences like this, and a whole lot of other activity, the clients knew the intruder was coming from the inside.

We had a great meal, but wrapped up quickly because we were eager to get back to the house. We were gone for about an hour. Once we returned and entered the home, we immediately heard a very loud bang coming from the second or third floor. It sounded like something heavy had just fallen over. Paul, one of our investigators, and I ran up to the second and third floors and did a quick sweep. Nothing seemed to be out of place. We hoped our recorders caught the sound to help us narrow down where it came from, but we couldn't immediately review the recorders. We were now curious to see if any other sounds were captured while we were gone. When we listened to the recordings during our investigation analysis on a later date, the recorders in the house picked up so much noise that it left my head spinning. It sounded like there was a party in the house while we were away. Heavy footsteps could be heard going up and down the steps and the sound of coins hitting the walls was recorded several times in different rooms and on different floors. Banging, knocking, and squeaking of dresser drawer handles were all picked up by the recorders, along with a variety of sounds from all three floors. We were certain that nobody was in the house because we had video cameras watching the doors and a good portion of the interior of the home was on camera. The only movement we saw was a quarter being thrown across the master bedroom, hitting a computer desk chair and dropping to the floor. Pretty amazing, considering no one was in the house!

It was time to start looking into some of the witness' claims, so we secured our clients in our controlled command area and began our physical investigation. It didn't take long before things started to happen. Virginia sat down quietly at the dining room table to try and "tune in" to what was going on. Within seconds, she started vigorously coughing and said she felt like someone tried to choke her but she got them off of her. We were hearing noises in all different rooms, wherever we were not. While our team members were watching the DVR camera monitor from command, they observed a second floor bedroom door close halfway. We responded and checked out the door. We didn't find anything that would have made it move on its own and propped it wide open against the wall again. A short time later, the door shut nearly all the way. Thinking maybe the door frame was off balance causing gravity to close it, we were suddenly proven wrong when the door opened back up, swinging the opposite way. So much for off balance! Not to mention, we had the door propped open from the last time. If this wasn't enough, the door did this two more times during the night. No unusual sounds appeared on our audio recorders, however. Later, when we reviewed this room on our DVR recording, we found that something that looked very much like a shadow of a human figure entered the room from the hallway and then quickly exited to the left where a wall would be. Could this have been the shadow figure the family had reported seeing? It sure looked like it to us. Nobody was in that area at the time and there was no way a shadow could have been made there. One thing for certain was that the clients seemed to be right. Something was going on this home, and in a big way!

At the conclusion of the investigation, Virginia felt that there were two spirits in this home and something a little more sinister. Virginia easily crossed over the two spirits. One, she felt, was an adult male who was mentally handicapped, and the other was his mother. Virginia felt the mother stayed in the home after she died, waiting for her husband to return from World War II, but he never did. The handicapped male stayed with her after he died because that was his mom and where he felt safe. Virginia believed the mother was the cause of much of the physical activity, such as the items being stacked on top of each other or thrown around the room. Virginia felt she was angry at the world because her husband left her to tend to her handicapped son by herself, and she now was taking it out on the new family living in the home. Once they were released, Virginia felt that a large amount of the physical activity would stop. This left only the sinister character to deal with. We later thought that this entity may have been the cause of the shadow we captured in the second floor bedroom. Virginia asked me to check with our clients to see if they had any type of Voodoo done to them or if they were playing around with Voodoo in some way. I thought to myself that this surely was going to make or break the medium in the eyes of the clients. That was a strange request to take to them and I wasn't sure how that was going to go, but it actually went better than I anticipated. The clients told me that they did believe they had some Voodoo done to them. The father of the home did, to be more specific, and apparently, some ill intentions from a former relationship that went bad was the reason.

They believed this woman sent something dark to him by the use of Santeria, which closely resembles Voodoo. Whether it worked, or he believed it worked, somehow something apparently became attached to this man and it would require a great deal more than the typical cleansing to eliminate. Virginia advised me that she was receiving impressions that this entity was negative in nature, not a demon, per se, but of a negative source. It was some type of negative creature sent to wreak havoc on the father and ruin him financially and physically, and it was. Virginia felt that a type of heart-binding ceremony was done on the father by this former relation. She also believed that the destructive events going on in the home, such as items being broken and things being thrown in the home were caused by this creature. The family never told us about this prior to our investigation because of personal issues surrounding the situation, but it was a major factor in the case.

The clients confirmed that they were losing money in their business and that the father had several minor heart attacks since the heart binding was done. He was only in his fifties at the time. Virginia felt we needed to revisit the home on another night, rather than trying to tackle it at this point. So, we scheduled another visit and would return with a plan in place to take on the sinister character causing the issues for the clients.

Our second visit was even more bizarre than the first, if that is possible. The clients showed us a picture of a black shadow figure they had captured on their cell phone camera since our first visit. It appeared to the father while in the kitchen and he was fast enough to snap a great picture, while being in a complete panic at the time. The figure in the picture was very similar to what we captured on our video camera in the second floor bedroom. I did everything I could to try and reproduce the shadow in the kitchen in order to rule out a natural cause for the anomaly, but I couldn't reproduce anything even remotely close to what was in the picture. The father actually became quite angry with me for trying to rule it out and I could see that he was genuinely upset and in fear of this thing, but we still had to look at alternate possibilities to rule the figure out or confirm that it was valid. It certainly appeared to be valid. The client understood that I still had a job to do and appreciated the fact that we considered it authentic after spending a great deal of time trying to debunk it. Paul had accompanied Virginia and me again for this second visit. While Virginia was talking with the clients, who were the only other two people in the home, in the kitchen, Paul and I decided to take a walk up to the third floor for a quick look. The third floor is divided into two small rooms, the front room, which was like a small library or sitting room and the back room, which had a drum set and a few other items in it. Paul and I chose to go into the front room first and sit for a few minutes. As soon as we sat down and got comfortable, I saw, and we both heard, a coin fly across the back room and hit the wall, then fall onto the floor. I immediately jumped to my feet, looking for the person who threw the coin. They certainly didn't come up or go down the stairs because we would have heard them. I looked in every crevice, but no one was there. When I went back and checked on the coin, I found a quarter lying on the floor and it was warm. The coin that hit the desk chair on our previous investigation was also a quarter. Was this significant? We weren't sure. Paul and I headed back downstairs and, this time, I wanted to remove the clients from the home altogether to see if there were any changes while they were out. Although I had seen more than enough to decide something paranormal was going on in this house, I still had some concerns that a human was also adding to the activity. I guess it was the cop in me!

With everyone out of the house except Paul, Virginia, and me, we could now get to work and really start digging in to what was going on there. We started in the basement, where the clients had reported that they recently had some wine bottles jumping off the wine rack and smashing on the floor. This was new since our last visit. We spent some time working in the basement, with not much occurring. Virginia wanted to play a recording of the "Hail Mary" prayer to see what would happen and turned on her CD player. Paul and I wanted to go spend more time on the third floor and left Virginia. After spending a few minutes by herself in the basement, Virginia witnessed a quarter falling out of thin air and hitting the concrete floor. Luckily, Paul had an urge to leave his camcorder running in the basement and caught it on camera. Virginia called for us to come down and we did a complete search of the ceiling area, which was unfinished, so it was just flooring and rafters, but we looked as well as we could to see if we could find a hole in the floor above us or hidden quarters, but we found nothing. No quarters, no holes, nothing! It appeared Mother Mary had some effect. I went to the living room above where the quarter had fallen from and did a complete search of the room. The floor was wall-to-wall carpeting and there were no vents, no cuts, or holes in the carpet anywhere. Not to mention, nobody else was in the house that could have pushed the quarter through even if there was a hole. So where did it come from? Maybe there was just one quarter on a beam that fell off by chance, we thought.

When we were satisfied no quarters could have been pushed through the floor into the basement from above and the boards were now checked for coins with none found, Paul wanted to spend some time alone in the basement. Virginia and I moved to the second floor. The camcorder was still running and Paul had spent about fifteen minutes there by himself with nothing happening. Paul, while trying to get something to respond, remarked to the empty room, while somewhat insulting his Polish heritage, "I'm here by myself. You have nothing to be afraid of with me. I'm just a big Pollock." Sure enough, a quarter fell out of thin air right in front of him and onto the concrete floor. Again! This time we knew there were no quarters anywhere on the ceiling and we caught it on camera for a second time. The case was getting stranger.

Paul and I decided that we were going to check out the master bedroom next. Virginia wanted to spend some more time just sitting and tuning in to the house. Paul and I climbed the staircase to the second floor and walked back the opposite direction, down the hallway, and into the master bedroom. I closed the bedroom door just far enough so I could still see the hallway and sat down on the bed. Paul and I talked casually for about three or four minutes when the bedroom door suddenly opened up nearly all the way, and then shut. Paul looked at me, I looked at Paul, shrugged my shoulders and I opened the door. There was no one there, but when I looked down, there were three quarters across the threshold of the doorway on the floor that we had just walked through. I just laughed and asked Paul if we were dealing with some kind of comedian or perhaps the spirit of a magician. How on Earth could quarters be appearing out of thin air and why? To this day, we are still not sure. However, Virginia feels it has something to do with the issue of the clients' financial disposition the Santeria was supposed to destroy, kind of an in your face type of insult via quarters to keep reminding them.

Virginia did a lot of cleansing work on the home and the client, but a lot more would have to be done by the client himself to break the connection with this negative entity. We would make one more visit to this home to finish up all that we could do for the family and, during our last visit, the production crew for The Haunted accompanied us to start filming for season two. It seemed our streak of crazy cases was not ending.

There is one thing I can say about this case, seeing is believing! This home was, and to this day still remains, the most physically active home that I have ever personally witnessed. This was the case that confirmed to me that paranormal activity is real. Oddly enough, even after this case, for me, the question still remained—Are ghosts real? Could they be the culprits causing all the activity at this home? Virginia definitely says they were. Or, is it possible that there is still some kind of strange environmental energy that we just don't know about yet

causing everything going on there? I was really starting to lean towards the possibility that ghosts were real
because much of the activity in this home seemed to be
responsive to where we were or what we were doing.
Virginia has been so accurate with her information, why
would I not believe her when she identifies ghosts as the
cause of activity? I was starting to! Either way, it was
definitely weird. What's even weirder was the amount
of bizarre cases that seemed to keep coming; if you consider finding human bones in your backyard bizarre,
that is!

Chapter 13

Preponderance of the Evidence

I don't know if it had something to do with the start of season two filming for *The Haunted* or if it was just fate, or coincidence, but The PPA seemed to be receiving a larger than normal amount of strange investigation requests. The production company wanted to use several of them for the show because they were different than the typical cases we normally worked on.

I received a phone call from a woman in Bangor, Pennsylvania, who was quite upset. It wasn't the activity in her house that was freaking her out so much as what she thought may have been the cause and not knowing what the eventual outcome would be. The clients had found bones in their backyard. Human bones! To make matters worse, one of their friends had crushed up what appeared to be a pelvic bone and threw it into the storm drain in front of their house. The second bone was a leg bone, which they took inside and preserved in their home. I'm not sure I would have brought it into my house, but to each their own.

When we responded and arrived at the home, we were taken on a quick walk-through of the property and the clients led us to the area where the bones were found. It was an area where the property bordered a very old cemetery. Many of the grave stones had been overgrown with brush near the backyard, but it looked like someone had cleaned it up at one point, creating a large debris pile of sticks and rock near the property line. There were obvious gopher holes around the debris pile, as well. This made for an interesting mix of possibilities as to whether the bones were going to be human or animal. As a criminal investigator, I have been called to many scenes where people believed they found human bones, but they turned out to be some sort of animal in almost every situation. In this case, we had a 50/50 shot, either the gophers dug up human remains or someone pitched some animal bones in the debris pile, and my bet was on animal. Until we could have the bone looked at to see if it was human or animal, we would deal with the activity in the house that the clients were reporting and see what we could find.

During the investigation, we had a little activity take place here and there, but nothing remarkable to speak of, until I spent some time in the basement with Virginia. After being in the basement for just a few minutes, I became rather comfortable there. It was an old, unfinished basement and kind of dark and creepy, but typically on investigations, once you get used to your surroundings, the creepiness goes away and you can then focus on your job.

The room was divided into two sections, a front room and a back room with a small doorway opening in between. We had walked back and forth between the two rooms a few times while Virginia was getting some general impressions. On the last pass from front to back, I had a really strong sensation of static electricity on my back and chills went up my spine. I told Virginia that I felt like, if I turned around, there was going to be someone standing right there. I did, but there wasn't. Virginia advised me that she felt like the spirit of the original owner of the house had just entered the basement with us. We continued on and spent a few minutes in the back room where Virginia kept receiving impressions of this man. Apparently, he was not happy that we were in his space and didn't care for us to be in the basement. Virginia asked me to go and sit on a set of concrete steps that led to the outside. They were covered by metal storm doors at the top.

I asked Virginia why she wanted me to do this, but she only said that she wanted to try something. Ok, so now I'm bait! *Why not*, I thought. I sat about three steps up with the doors just above my head. Virginia asked me to close my eyes, take a deep breath, and invite the man to come closer to me. As I asked the man to come closer in my thoughts, I heard something hard hit the doors right above me and fall to the ground at my feet. I opened my eyes and asked what that was that just hit the doors. It was a small stone.

Virginia began laughing and I asked what was so funny. I assumed that I was the target of a bad joke since Virginia asked me to sit in the dark with my eyes closed as something was thrown at me, but Virginia swore to me that she did not do anything. Virginia said she felt that the area of the stairs was where the man would hang out and smoke, his personal space. She wanted me to sit in his spot to see if there would be any reaction from him. Obviously there was! A small stone was apparently thrown at me, but I still wasn't buying the fact that it wasn't Virginia. Lucky for her, I had a camcorder sitting right on my lap looking right at her. When I replayed the recording, you could plainly see that Virginia never moved. The stone could be seen flying through the air coming right at me, but where it came from, who knows. Virginia maintains that the man threw it at me. All I can say is that I know it wasn't her. Al, a third investigator who was with us in the basement, was also recording Virginia at the time and she never moved. Al was in an area where the stone could not have come from, so we know it wasn't him. It was a very strange occurrence indeed, and another great case for the books.

If you're curious about the bone, we took it to an anthropology lab at a local university, where it was examined by several doctors. The lab was also a wildlife research lab so it offered us the best chance of identifying what the bone belonged to. It took a few days, but I finally got a phone call from my contact. The analysis was complete, the results were in, and the final conclusion—the bone was human!

Now, that I didn't expect, but as I already mentioned, it was a 50/50 shot. This was the first time I've had to bring a county coroner into a case. It was determined that the most likely cause for the appearance of the bones were from gophers. Back when the cemetery was developed, many people were buried in wooden caskets. Over time, the caskets would rot. The creepy part was, the bones were most likely dug up from one of many unmarked graves that were well into the clients' backyard, but they had no idea they were even there. Virginia had received impressions during her initial walk-through that there were graves in the backyard that were no longer marked or never marked at all.

We later found out that, historically, families that could not afford a nice stone would have their decedents buried in the back of the cemetery with no markers. Over time, the property lines had moved and what was now the clients' backyard was once part of the cemetery. To go one step further, we brought in a ground penetrating radar team to verify Virginia's impressions and, sure enough, she was right! There were graves in the family's backyard.

Our team moved on to another great case. It was a three-hundred-year-old, three-story colonial home with the original fieldstone finish on the outside of the house in the small community of Mohnton, Pennsylvania. It seems the family was seeing several apparitions in various rooms of the house. They had captured their own recordings of unexplainable noises in the attic. Two family dogs would stare at "nothing" and then react like someone was there. The clients reported various objects had moved on their own in the home. They reported hearing voices and seeing shadows in the hallway outside the bedrooms on the third floor throughout the night. Along with that, many other personal experiences, such as having the feeling that they are being watched and even being poked or having their hair tugged on as they sat watching TV were being reported to us. It was a great mix of physical, visual, and audible events.

Upon Virginia's arrival and during our initial walk-through, Virginia gave one of the most detailed and accurate initial readings that I have observed. She was able to narrow one event down to the right family member, out of the five that were present, who was sitting in a specific chair when it happened, in a specific room, watching TV, and having their ear tugged on. Pretty amazing accuracy on that bit of info, I must admit! Most significantly, though, was that Virginia picked up on a male who would walk through the third floor hallway at night and then go into the attic. He was not happy with people being in that area. The clients had told us that they had a local paranormal team come in to investigate before contacting The PPA and, near the end of their investigation, one of their investigators was leaving the attic and heard a loud growl and was physically pushed. That team was able to document the activity in the home for the clients, but did not have the resources to resolve the haunting and that is why they called in our team.

During the investigation, our members had several personal experiences that completely backed up the claims of the clients. Nearly everyone, except yours truly, of course, had some type of experience where they were either poked at or tugged on, mostly occurring in the living room, the master bedroom or the attic. These were the three areas wherein the clients had reported having similar physical contact. We were able to record several unusual sounds in the attic and first floor and documented a few EVPs.

After the investigation had concluded and we were able to review our recordings, we found an amazing video clip from the viewpoint of the master bedroom looking into the hallway. This was the area that the clients had reported seeing figures walking past their closed doors during the night. The bedroom doors were louvered in the middle, wide enough to see into the dimly lit hallway at night, even though the doors were closed. This was the same area that Virginia picked up on similar activity and where the children in another room, down the hall, had also reported seeing the same. Our video camera monitoring this area of the hallway captured what appeared to be a figure going back and forth through a laser grid that we had projecting onto the hallway wall. No distinct shape could be identified, but the laser grid completely darkened in different areas, from left to right and then right to left, at different speeds and at different heights.

Whatever the clients were seeing in that hallway seemed to have been captured by our cameras. According to Virginia, it was the spirit of a man who was somehow summoned there when prior residents of the home used a Ouija Board, or something similar, to try and find out who was haunting the house many years ago.

The home was cleared of all but one female spirit who loved the home as much as the new family and liked watching over the mother of the house. This spirit wanted to stay and, with the client's blessing, was invited to remain there with the family and continue on with her life on the other side, whatever that may be. Hopefully, it was a happy ending for everyone involved on both sides!

Between our regularly scheduled cases, members of The PPA were invited to attend a lecture at a Catholic church where an Exorcist, trained in Rome, was coming to speak. It was rare that an exorcist would identify himself as such and even more unique that he would talk about exorcisms, especially in the church. A small contingency of The PPA investigators were interested in what he had to say and I certainly wasn't going to pass up this opportunity to go, so we did. During his lecture, the exorcist spoke more on preventative measures of how to live a good, possession free life, but a small portion of the speech did cover a few of his experiences during exorcisms. Pretty amazing stories to hear! I came out of this event with an incredible experience myself, but it had nothing to do with the information I had just learned about or anything to do with the exorcist himself. It was more about what had happened while the lecture was taking place and something that happened to me.

My crew had picked two rows of pews to sit in, about six or seven sections back from the front row. No one sat in front of us, so we had a great view of the Priest. About halfway through the lecture, as I was focused on the Priest, he suddenly went blurry. I rubbed my eyes because it gave me the feeling that I had some mucus or tears in the way, but nothing changed. Now distracted by the blurry vision, I looked away from the Priest to my right and focused on a fixture across the room. The blurriness went away. Problem solved! I looked back at the Priest and my sight was blurry again. *What the heck was going on here,* I thought. I looked away again, clear! I looked back, blurry! It took me a few rounds of doing this, but I finally realized it wasn't my eyes. There was a small section about four pews ahead of us, about two feet wide and three feet high, that was blurry. Clear to the left and clear to the right. Whatever it was, it was right in front of us and blurring my view of the priest. The best way I can describe what I was observing is a two foot wide by three feet high area of something, above the top of the pew, that looked like heat rising from hot blacktop on a sunny day. After trying to wipe my eyes clean again a few times, it was gone.

Thinking I was losing it, I kept it to myself at the church and on the ride home, until Paulette, one of our attending members who rode there with me, said, "I wasn't going to say anything, but I want to tell you about something weird that happened to me in the church." My heart started racing. I told her that before she said anything to me, I wanted to know if she saw something. She said she did. I asked her if it was something blurry a few pews ahead of us and directly in the view of the Priest.

Paulette hit me in the arm with pure amazement and exclaimed, "Yes!"

Holy crap, I thought! It wasn't just me! I asked Paulette what she thought it was and she said she didn't know. Neither did I, but it was weird. I called Virginia the next day and told her about our exciting encounter. Virginia very matter of factually said, it was probably just a spirit. Apparently, she saw several there with us that night, but that's normal for her, so she didn't say anything. Ok, I thought, just a spirit then. That solves it. Wait... what...?

Our team was back on the road soon after, off to our next investigation. We were headed to a beautiful hotel in East Windham, New York. The view from the top of the mountain was breathtaking. As strange cases go, this was yet another one to add to our books. The clients purchased the hotel to hold various spiritual events and to accommodate visitors to the great ski area they were located near. They spent a lot of time updating the hotel, but after being there for a while, they started noticing a very bad smell in Room 12. Foul, to put it bluntly, but they could not account for the source. They looked for dead rodents, cleaned the air ducts, and even went so far as to gut the whole room—floors, walls, and ceiling was replaced with new everything. The smell had left for a few weeks and they thought they had the problem solved, but the smell came back. Clients would even complain about the stench from time to time. It would come and go, unlike having a dead animal in the wall that would smell constantly. To make things even worse, the TV started to turn on and off by itself, people were hearing voices, and the personalities of people who stayed in Room 12 seemed to change while they were staying there. The clients were becoming concerned.

By chance, on one afternoon during lunch in the hotel's restaurant, a visitor, who had been present for a conversation about the activity in the room, asked the owners if it had something to do with the murder that happened in Room 12 years ago. Reportedly, this was where a girl was killed, only to be discovered days later. The owners were startled. They had never heard of a murder in the hotel and the woman identified the same room number where the activity was taking place. The owners never mentioned what room they were having trouble with for this woman to hear. Now, loaded with stories of a murder, they were off to research the history of the hotel and felt that maybe something paranormal was causing the activity and the foul smell. That's when The PPA got involved. Our Historical Research Director, Kelly, joined the search for proof of a murder. Unfortunately, she had about as much luck as the owners. Many people in this community had heard about a murder taking place at the hotel, but nothing was found to be documented anywhere. No news clipping, no police reports, and no records of death on file anywhere. It was becoming a real life murder mystery.

When I spoke with the clients about the case, I was very interested in their theory about someone dying in the hotel room and that possibly being the cause for some sort of phantom rotting corpse smell. Could that be possible? Falling back on my police experience, I thought the best way I could dismiss the possibility of a corpse, or ghost corpse, would be to call in a trained cadaver dog team to help investigate. If the dogs did not indicate that there was a corpse present at some point in time, I could possibly rule out a murder and the theory of a rotting corpse. Dogs can pick up the scent of a corpse from over 100 years ago, in some instances, so it was worth a try. Additionally, the search team would bring in a control dog that was not trained to alert on the presence of a corpse, but would show interest if there was a rodent dead somewhere in the floor or wall. It all sounded logical to me. The search team was on board and a date was scheduled for their visit. I wanted to keep their investigation separate from ours, however, so we would not contaminate any information that Virginia was coming up with and vice versa.

The search team arrived at the hotel on the scheduled date and we did some preliminary ground work. I passed along important background information that they needed to conduct a successful search of the second floor. The team brought two cadaver dogs and a third dog, which acted as their non-cadaver control dog. The team was ready and began their search of the second floor, utilizing one dog at a time so as not to be distracted by each other. Emy, the first dog handler, moved her dog down the hall, working door to door to see if there was any interest on the dog's part to go into any particular rooms.

As we got to Room 12, the dog mildly indicted that she wanted to enter the room. Emy worked her way past the door to the end of the hallway with no other interest areas shown by the dog. Emy brought her dog back to Room 12 and entered. An initial run through of the room was done with the dog, and then a second pass was made where the dog would be searching for any signs of a cadaver. When the dog got to the back corner of the left side of the room, she gave a mild indication that a body may have been in that area. The dog showed no interest in any other areas of the room, but kept trying to get on the bed against Emy's wishes. The dog actually made it on the bed a few times, only to be ordered down by her handler. Emy explained to me that her dog is trained not to do that unless ordered to and found it odd behavior for the dog.

As we were preparing to the leave the room, the dog jumped up on me with her paws on my shoulders, trying to work her way towards the TV that was mounted on the wall right next to my head. This was the same TV that the owners reported turning on and off by itself. Emy pulled the dog down, apologized, and told me she's never done that before. Animals in haunted locations often exhibit strange behavior. Was this behavior by the dog part of what was going on, or did the dog just really like me, or want to watch TV?

With one possible area of interest found by the first dog in Room 12, it was time to bring in the second dog with her handler, Bruce. This dog was more seasoned and hopefully would give us a clearer indication, one way or another, if a cadaver actually had been present in Room 12. The same search procedure was followed and, when the dog approached Room 12, she gave a solid indication that she wanted to enter the room. During the search of the room, the dog gave a very strong indicator that there was a body in the back, left corner of the room, exactly where the first dog had shown interest. A dog cannot tell if a body is currently present or present at some other point in the past. They alert on specific proteins left behind by rotting human bodies, and both dogs did just that in the same spot. I asked Bruce what that meant and he told me with a great deal of certainty that, at some point in time, there was a body in that location. I was dumbfounded. My plan to dismiss the idea that there could have been a body in that room just went down the toilet. Now it appeared that the possibility of there being a body in Room 12 was a reality. This was going to make my work a little more interesting.

To make things more bizarre, Bruce's dog began trying to get up on the bed just like the first dog and finally Bruce let her. Bruce told me his dog should not be doing that, but she was finding something of interest there. What it was, we don't know. The dogs have the ability to search for living bodies, as well, but since there was nobody present there, the dog shouldn't have been either. We decided to add it to the strange and uncertain category that seemed to be growing. Before Bruce would make his final decision regarding what the dogs were alerting to, he wanted to run the control dog through the area, just to be certain we weren't dealing with a dead animal. The cadaver dogs will ignore a dead animal for the most part, but a control dog should show interest. The control dog was run through the second floor, failing to alert on the door to Room 12 as he passed. He was taken into Room 12 and, with several passes made along the walls, the dog showed more interest in going back out into the hallway than in anything in the room. With that, it appears as if we had ourselves a body! Sort of! So would our medium find the same?

During our physical investigation, Virginia began, as always, with a walk-through of the building. This was a particularly big building, so it was taking a little bit longer than usual. When Virginia got to the second floor of the hotel, she started walking down the hallway toward the end of the building where Room 12 was located. Virginia was not told what or where the activity was at this point, so the closer she got to Room 12, the more my heart started beating in anticipation of seeing if she would pick up on that particular room as the problem area. Virginia was going back and forth, touching the doors to several of the rooms on the right and left side of the hallway as she walked and eventually approached Room 12. As she moved in front of the door, she tapped it with her hand. I thought, yes, she got it, but then she continued walking right by. Bummer, my fun meter just hit zero!

She kept going and put her hand on the next door down the hallway, turned around and walked right back to Room 12 and said, "I don't like the feeling in this room," and walked in. No freaking way, I exclaimed! She did get it! Virginia told us that she felt there was activity going back and forth between Room 12 and the next room down, but primarily in Room 12.

My head had barely stopped spinning before Virginia began relating impressions of a young woman who was in the room. The woman was going back and forth between Room 12 and Room 10 in a panic. Virginia said the girl died in Room 12, but that wasn't supposed to happen. Virginia became very upset and said she was picking up the girl's emotions and how the girl died. Virginia explained that the girl was in the room with a man. They were both using heroin and the girl became ill. The man injected her with one last dose of heroin and the girl went into a panic. She knew something was wrong and died right there in the corner of the room. Virginia pointed to the same exact spot where the two cadaver dogs had indicated there was a body. She began to tear up and said she was seeing some blood loss from the girl and she kept yelling at Virginia that it wasn't supposed to happen. Virginia, experiencing the emotions of this girl, kept telling us that she was trying to calm the girl down, but was having a hard time. She said the girl was scared and still in a panic because there was a man there trying to interfere with what Virginia was doing. The man did not want Virginia getting involved and was trying to block her from the girl. Since Virginia was visibly upset and taking on the emotions of this poor girl, I told her we were taking a break and leaving the room.

I removed the team to the lobby of the hotel and reviewed in my mind what had just happened. Just like the owners had mentioned about people taking on a different personality while they were in the room, Virginia seemed to be picking up extreme emotions from the girl there. She also pointed out the same exact spot that the dogs hit on. It was a lot to take in and I was amazed to say the least. My whole theory of dismissing the stench as a rotting corpse, or some type of paranormal association with a rotting corpse, was now completely out the window. Not only had the dogs confirmed a body had been in Room 12 at some point in time, but Virginia just independently confirmed that for us, as well, and with a whole lot more detail than the dogs provided. Virginia gets the treat this time! In the end, it appears as if an accidental heroin overdose had occurred and at someone else's hand. This wasn't quite a murder, but it doesn't get much closer than that to being one. It was still a mystery as to why we couldn't find any documentation on the death, but in the strange and secretive world of drug addiction, it may have been covered up. Virginia felt that the girl's body was dumped somewhere and never found.

When it was time to do the cleansing of the building and try to release the girl, Virginia went right to work, starting at the center of it all in Room 12. Virginia sat at a small table and began to pray. She had asked the trapped girl to come closer to her. She felt the girl was still very excited, but Virginia was able to calm her down to a point that she could work with her, at least. Virginia told us that she was getting some resistance from the male who was also present, but felt that after the girl left, he would most likely go on his own, too. As she continued with her work, a strange thing occurred. My face became extremely hot, almost like standing next to a large camp fire. I had the sensation that I wanted to pull back to avoid the heat. Because Virginia was right in the middle of what she was doing, I didn't want to interrupt, so I stuck it out and didn't say anything.

When she was done and felt that the girl had finally gone, I talked about the sensations I was feeling during her cleansing. Nicole, another PPA investigator present with me in the room, told us that she also was feeling heat and her ears became really hot. Virginia explained that it was the energy from the process that just took place as she released the girl. I don't know what it was, but it was another extraordinary experience for us all as we wrapped up the case. Not to mention, having a cadaver dog team on a paranormal investigation whose findings corroborated with the psychic's—amazing! What a great learning experience for us all. I am not sure if I believe that the foul smell the owners were reporting was that of a rotting body, but I will admit, there was some type of connection to the activity in Room 12. Weeks after the cleansing, the clients told me that there was no further activity in the hotel room and the horrible smell had not returned. I pray this poor girl is now at peace!

By now you may be thinking that I have a pretty firm belief that ghosts are real. In civil court, there is something referred to as a "Preponderance of the Evidence." Unlike criminal court, where it takes a whole lot of evidence to prove a case in most instances, a preponderance of the evidence is just enough evidence to make it more likely than not that the fact you are trying to prove is true. I certainly will concede that a preponderance of the evidence seems to exist when it comes to the investigations I have been involved in. The problem is, I'm a criminal investigator who deals with criminal court cases, and criminal court cases require more evidence. I'm conditioned to look for evidence. I can't help but wonder, even with all that I've seen up until now, could there still be something I'm missing here. Is paranormal activity caused by ghosts, spirits, entities, or whatever you want to refer to them as, or is the energy that causes paranormal activity also making people believe there are ghosts present?

I am reminded of a case wherein the family was reporting all kinds of activity, including witnessing a small child roaming through the home at different points in time. Our team that night included Jim, an investigator who I consider one of our super skeptics. Jim, like me, is open to the possibility that ghosts may exist, but needs to see the hard core evidence to make him a believer. He is even tougher on this matter than I am. The great thing about Jim is, even though he doesn't really believe in ghosts at this point, he is still willing to help out Virginia with her metaphysical work in any way she needs in order to assist the family.

During this investigation, while Virginia was speaking with the clients in the kitchen, Jim was helping me with the setup of our stationary cameras. I was in an upstairs bedroom, while Jim was in the living room making some adjustments and called out to me. I called back to Jim and he asked me who had just came up the stairs and walked down the hallway. As far as I knew, nobody had. I went to where Jim was and he told me that he just watched a little girl walk up the stairs, turn, and go down the hallway. This really wasn't unexpected or too out of the ordinary because there were two kids living in the home and they hadn't left yet. But when Jim walked into the kitchen to find the two children standing there, it left him a bit bewildered. The biggest skeptic we had on our team has now seen something. The funny part is, he won't admit that it was a ghost.

After reflecting on it for a few minutes, Jim still held the possibility open that it was just his mind playing tricks on him because he knew, coming into the case, that there were reports of seeing a child in the house. It's tough to sway a skeptic sometimes, but it did cast doubt about ghosts into my mind because, if he saw something so clearly and was still not convinced that it was a ghost, could everyone else who wants to believe just be accepting an illusion based on their internal thinking. I have been on many more cases than Jim and I still have not seen anything that I could definitely call a ghost. Jim has seen something most people would consider a ghost and he thinks it may have been nothing. Is preponderance of the evidence enough? I had to think more on this.

Chapter 14

Chasing Shadows

I have worked on well over 100 resolution cases during my time investigating. Some of the more experiential cases, I have presented here for you. The majority of the investigations have very little or no physical activity while we are there and are often, at times, very quiet and sometimes downright boring. It's not quite like you see on TV, where the highlights of the investigations are consolidated into a half hour show. Much of the evidence we find is discovered after the on-site investigation has been completed, during our review period.

Some locations have had pretty wild activity on a Friday night and then absolutely no activity on Saturday, so it's very hard to tell what will happen, or when something might happen, on any given case. Many clients also report that activity comes and goes, much like the seasons that our lives cycle through each year. There are times of excitement and times of rest. For the most part, I have experienced very physical activity, such as doors opening and closing or coins being thrown across a room, but there were a few instances when I can say that I did see or hear something that I would consider a ghost.

Our team was requested to investigate the home of a nurse who had recently been in a bad car accident and, soon after, started having some activity in her home. Since this accident was the only major event that happened recently in her life, it seemed like a pretty strong trigger for the activity to start after living in the home with no activity for so many years. Either the trauma from the accident opened her psychically and she was able to pick up on whoever was in her house or something attached itself to her after the accident.

When a person has some type of trauma, it is believed by many metaphysical practitioners that it can damage their aura and open them psychically or make them noticeable to the other side. This seemed to be the case for this woman, according to Virginia. After her aura was damaged from the accident, it appears that she caught the attention of a spirit that had been at the hospital where she worked and it followed her home. The woman began to "feel" when the spirit was in the room, and that feeling increased to the point that she started seeing shadows.

When we arrived at the house, Virginia instantly picked up on who the woman felt was there. We had done a little investigating throughout the home, but there really wasn't much going on. Virginia and I had later taken a rotation downstairs in the finished basement. It was a room with no windows, so it was very dark except for some ambient light coming from the staircase. I had taken up a position leaning against the back of a couch and Virginia was standing in the middle of the room facing me. Virginia was casually talking to me about the day's events and that's when I saw a whitish-gray light, about a foot wide and five feet in height, go from my right to left directly behind her. It was about the same height as Virginia. At first thought, I just assumed it was the light from a car going by, but then I realized there were no windows in the room. I didn't say anything about it, but Virginia then broke from her conversation and told me that there was an energy that just moved from her left to right (opposite me while she was facing me), and then went right back into her conversation like nothing happened. Whoa, whoa, whoa, hold up there, Virginia! I stopped her and asked about this energy she had just nonchalantly informed me of. She said it was a male figure, the same one that she was picking up on the first floor, which we believe was also the shadow the client kept seeing, and I saw it, too! It didn't look like a figure to me, just a beam of light, and it was fast. Virginia told me what I just saw was the man and congratulated me on actually seeing something. I'll admit it was pretty cool, and to have someone else verify that I saw something was great.

I have learned along the way that when people claim to have seen a ghost, it may not actually always be what you think a ghost should look like. The idea of a ghost in my mind may be different than what you think a ghost should look like, but it usually appears human looking and transparent. After talking to hundreds of clients and other witnesses that believe they encountered a ghost, I found out that there were many different sightings that people placed into the ghost category. Obviously, the number one image that people see, which makes them think they saw a ghost, is a figure in human form. Sometimes, people report seeing a solid figure, just as if you or I were standing there in front of them, but other times witnesses report seeing transparent, translucent or even partial apparitions. I'm not sure what I'd think if I only saw half a spirit and I'm not sure how to explain why only half of a spirit would appear, unless they were cut in half, perhaps, but let's not go there!

There are also witnesses who claim to see black masses. They are sometimes in the form of a human shape, but not always. What is interesting is that almost all of the people who witness these black featureless figures report them to be extremely dark in nature with the complete absence of light, almost like a void. I think that is why so many people are fearful when they see them. They can be very frightening, and we generally associate darkness with evil. An interesting side note, if you think about it, you can't measure darkness. You can only measure light, or how little, or a complete absence of light, but it is always the light that we are measuring. There is no measurement for darkness. There is no "negative" when it comes to darkness, such as you find with temperature. There is just darkness. If spirits are thought of as light beings, maybe that's why some people feel so afraid, because they see an absence of that light in a being, such as a black mass. If it is not of the light, where is it from?

Many of the people we talk to report seeing various types of cohesive mist that free flows through an area, staying together as a whole as it moves, but often times changing shape. These mists appear out of nowhere and often disappear as fast as they appear. I can understand how observing mist formations outside, especially on a damp or humid night, will lead people to confuse condensation in the air with mist figures. The mist may not necessarily be seen with the naked eye, but once a picture is taken, it shows up very well in pictures due to the bright flash of the camera. What is harder to grasp is how these mist figures spontaneously appear in dry homes and other buildings, especially if there is no steam heat in the building. To make it more complicated, people sometimes report seeing the mist in shades of gray or blue.

At a job The PPA was working on in Scranton, Pennsylvania, we had set up two laser grids that projected against the second floor hallway wall at the top of the stairs and against the wall inside the master bedroom. Two of our investigators, Nicole and Paulette, were on a rotation in that area. Paulette was stationary in the hall and Nicole was in the master bedroom, sitting on the bed. I was at our command area monitoring our cameras. Something happened and I could see Paulette react to it. She started looking in the direction of the master bedroom. About two seconds later, Nicole had a similar reaction and started looking away from the master bedroom door, towards the front wall. Both started moving around the areas they were in, looking for something. The two investigators then got together and had a conversation.

I radioed to ask what was going on and they both reported seeing some type of a mist moving through the air that could be seen within the laser light itself as the laser reflected off of it. It moved from left to right, as if something came up the stairs and went into the master bedroom. Nicole told me that it went past her and disappeared. Monitoring from command, I did not see anything unusual on the cameras in that area, but the reactions, first from Paulette and then immediately after by Nicole, certainly indicated to me that there was something out of the ordinary going on and that neither of them realized the other had seen something until they discussed it together. To them, it appeared to be the same type of mist anomaly that many people report seeing. Was it a ghost? Neither of them could confirm that.

One of the most highly observed phenomenon is that of a shadow or shadow figure. Sometimes similar in appearance to a black mass, these shadows are somewhat transparent and not so dark and ominous in nature.

This, by far, is the most common sighting reported by clients. A large majority of the reports include clients seeing something out of the corner of their eye, but claim it was there long enough to see it move across a room or up a set of stairs. Others have watched these mysterious shadows head on as they move slowly through a space. Many people report that the shadows will pass by a nightlight, TV, or window and block out the light as they pass. I don't know too many shadows that will block out a light. To me, this suggests that, if what the observers are seeing is real, it has to have some type of mass, or some way to absorb or reflect the light. I often think that because many people are predisposed to believe that they have activity in their home, legitimate or not, their minds may cause them to think they just saw a shadow figure instead of recognizing whatever just happened for what it really is (Ghost Effect). However, I also believe that what some people are seeing is real, because I've seen it myself.

There have been many cases where I have seen something dark, like a shadow, move quickly across a room or along a wall and I couldn't find any explanation for what would have caused it. Sometimes I think it may be just my eyes playing tricks on me, or light play from outside, but there are those rare occasions where I have seen a shadow move across a room and block out the light as it passed something illuminated. We do our best to try and recreate these shadows, or find a cause, whether it originated from a source inside or whether there was something outside that could have caused the event.

In most cases, we do find realistic explanations. Other times, we are left with the same questions as the client. In either event, we do our best to try and track down the source of all of these shadows. You would be surprised at just how difficult that is to do sometimes. In smaller homes located in very rural areas, you can sometimes get to the cause very quickly if it is a naturally caused shadow. When you're at a three story, 600,000 square foot building nearly the size of a city block with a ton of open space, plenty of windows and street traffic in a fairly populated area, it gets more complicated. If you feel that your clients are credible, and they are adamant that they have activity, you want to do your very best to help them, after all, that is why you are there. You have to look at every report, every sighting, every concern, and you can easily spend the entire night chasing shadows, coming so close to finding what you are looking for and, just when you think you have it, it's gone!

Chapter 15

The Living Are Scarier than the Dead

I am often asked at public appearances and lectures if I am ever afraid to go on investigations or what the scariest location was to investigate. I remember the very first time I was asked one of those questions. It took me a few seconds to respond. I hadn't really thought about it before.

When I first began my work in this field, I had some expected anxiety about attending my very first case, but I found out quickly that it wasn't what I had thought it would be, and the anxiety went away. From then on, I've approached each individual case from a very objective point of view. There is usually so much technical preparation going on that I really don't pay too much attention to what could happen on a case and just deal with things as they come up, if they even come up at all. Unfortunately, I have the privilege of being a full time criminal investigator, investigating major crimes against people. What I should say is, it really is a privilege to have that position, but criminal investigators, along with other positions in law enforcement, have to experience things that the people who are not in that field wouldn't want to know about or deal with, and it certainly leaves a big emotional impact on those who do this work. Individuals who have the opportunity to work in both the criminal and paranormal fields will most likely tell you, with great conviction, that the living are far scarier than the dead. Once you know why I say this, you can see just how silly the question is.

In order to fully explain this, and for you to completely understand my point of view, I am stepping far away from the reality that TV presents to you for a moment and dismissing the sensationalism of what ghosts and hauntings are made out to be. I am giving you the cold, hard, and completely cruel truth of what actually is when we are talking about life and death. I will offer you warning that I will not sugar coat what I am going to say. It is what it is! I have always lived by those words and I feel it is important for me to explain what I feel is the most important thing to know about ghosts, from my perspective, and that becomes the foundation of my inevitable response to people when I'm asked if I have ever been scared on a case. I am going to share some unsettling experiences with you that I have had to be a part of throughout my years as a police officer. Some may find this upsetting. However, my intent is not to upset anyone, but rather to give a clear understanding of why I think the way I do. If you are a sensitive person, please feel free to skip ahead to the next chapter.

As all Troopers start out when they graduate from a State Police Academy, I was assigned to a uniformed patrol unit. It's a very proud time for new Troopers, making it through a very intensive boot camp and basic training period. The training is extensive, but one thing that they can't teach you is how to emotionally handle some of the incidents that we respond to. Hearing about it is one thing, however, arriving on a scene and seeing the sights and smelling the smells, dealing with victims and families of victims is something that you, with little preparation, are immediately hit in the face with, and you have to find your own way to deal with it as best you can. As a patrol Trooper, you respond to nearly all incidents, whether minor or major, so you witness it all. Unfortunately, much of what we experience is unpleasant.

The largest number of unpleasant incidents that patrol Troopers have to respond to are motor vehicle accidents. They can be just as stressful as murders because violent car accidents can leave some real damage on a victim's body that most people don't care to see. I, like every other officer, have responded to head-on car crashes, roll overs, ejections and multiple vehicle accidents. I have seen people with severe lacerations, bodies crushed and torn in half, limbs ripped off and, most disturbingly, people who have been decapitated. There is a certain smell that sticks with you from these accidents and, unless you were there, you probably wouldn't even think of that. To see a torn up body is one thing, but someone still has to remove it from the scene, whether it be all tangled in a car, or under a truck, or wherever else a body may rest. The County Coroner is in charge of victim removal, but as investigators, part of our duty is to assist the coroner. I have had the unpleasant experience of shoveling brains off of a roadway and into a bag more than once in my career. They didn't warn me about that in the academy.

When I was assigned to a criminal investigation unit, the gruesomeness took on a whole new meaning. As part of my new duty requirement as a detective, I was assigned to investigate all types of deaths. I think most people can understand that sometimes accidents just happen and people die in vehicle crashes. When you are investigating non-traffic related deaths, it usually deals with a more senseless component to the death that affect people differently, including drug overdose deaths, homicides, suicides, and what I like to sometimes refer to as "death by stupidity."

I don't like to make light of someone's death, however if you are going to try and steal copper wire from a factory in order to scrap it for drug money, make sure the power is off first. Yeah, that happened—death by stupidity! Life's natural selection at work, you might say. Regardless of the level of intelligence, that man was still someone's son and guess who gets to go and notify the family of his death—the police. Something no police officer likes to do is death notifications. We often have to tell families that their loved one has died but, unlike accidents, there is a feeling of pointlessness to many of the deaths we investigate. Most are not accidents and didn't have to happen. Once the news is delivered, you sometimes become an immediate grief counselor and reactions can become extreme. You can't drop a bomb on someone and just walk out. Many times we, as investigators, have to spend some time talking with families and answering questions the best we can before our departure. That part is often more emotionally taxing than dealing with the incident itself.

I could never understand the draw toward heroin, especially since there is so much information out there on how addictive it is, but teenagers and young adults still continue to become addicted users. In so many cases of heroin use, I've investigated the deaths of young people. This is one of the most pointless deaths there is. It can be totally avoided if people would just stay away from the damn stuff. It makes me angry every time I have to investigate an overdose death because the dead person is the cause of my distress when I have to be the one to talk with their grieving family. Nobody likes to be in that position and I hate making people sad. I have my own family and I dislike going home in a bad mood. One investigation in particular that stands out for me centered around a twenty-six-year-old male who had been fighting with his parents about his drug abuse. He left the argument and went to his friend's house for the night. His friends were also heroin users. Ironically, he died that same night from the very thing he had just been fighting with his parents about. Just prior to wrapping up the victim in a body bag, his "friend" asked if he could have the victim's gold rings to remember him by. The cold truth of the matter was that his friend wanted the rings to go cash in for money to buy more heroin. Compassionate guy, right? Unfortunately, that is the cold truth about the drug world. If you haven't met a heroin addict, the compassionate human element completely disappears from them and they become animals hunting down the means for their next fix. It usually doesn't matter how they get it, as long as they get it. It's very sad!

Although death by stupidity, a category I also include drug overdoses in, are upsetting on a certain level, though they are no match for suicides and homicides. Without getting too graphic, it's amazing what a shot gun will do to someone's head. Why people who kill themselves decide to do it inside a home is beyond me. It is one of the most selfish and hurtful things they can do to their loved ones. I realize people are suffering and want their physical or emotional pain to end and I won't judge them for that, but it saddens me to see the after-effects bear down on the ones who love them. Not only do they have to deal with the death of their loved one, but they now also have to clean up the mess. The coroner's office will take away the body and any body parts, but they don't clean the scene. It is up to the family to mop up all the blood, sometimes from the floor, or the wall, and even the ceiling. When you hear about a suicide, or that someone shot themselves in the head, you probably don't think about that, do you? Trust me, it can be messy and it has a lasting effect on everyone involved, especially the family. One of the most disturbing suicides I have had to investigate was that of a fourteen-year-old girl who hung herself from a tree in a field behind her house. This was a girl who wanted to die for some time and had written poetry about it, almost like it was her destiny. She was in counseling for months and had two prior failed attempts, but this time, she was successful. To me, there is nothing more disturbing than seeing a hanging victim, especially one so young. I don't know why, maybe it's the way that their face looks or the way their body unnaturally hangs, but, for me, it's just upsetting to have to see. I feel bad for the family members who find them, as it is hard to get the image out of your mind. Would that be the way you want to remember your loved one?

Murders are a whole different kind of animal. You don't truly know evil until you see what one human being can do to another. I was involved in an investigation years ago wherein a young man had killed his girlfriend by shooting her right in the face with a shotgun in their small apartment bedroom. He then turned the gun on himself and blew his head off. Well, most of it, anyway. It was one of the bloodiest crime scenes I have witnessed. I was assigned another case wherein a husband became separated from his wife. She was seeing another man and the husband wanted her to come back home. During the estranged wife's visit to the husband's house one night, and after several failed attempts to win her heart back, the husband shot his wife right in the forehead and later told me that it was because he "loved her so much." That makes sense, right? On yet another incident, I investigated a murder wherein a son beat his father to death by hitting him repeatedly with a flashlight on the head. To make it worse, he then wrapped his father in a tarp and dumped his body over an embankment in a trash pile to rot in the summer heat for weeks. His body was eventually found. Nothing says love like dumping dad in a garbage pile!

The worst thing about a body being at a location for days or weeks, depending on the time of year, is that an ominous odor begins to appear. It is similar to that of a rotting deer carcass along the side of a roadway, but worse. Once you smell it, you never forget it! Bodies decompose as part of the natural life process, but it's not pretty. If you have ever wondered why there are so many black flies that seem to be everywhere, or what their purpose in life can possibly be, besides making your garbage can gross, it is to help move the decomposition process along. One thing a decomposing body attracts is flies. Flies lay eggs, eggs turn into maggots, and maggots eat flesh. Until you have seen a rotting body being eaten away by thousands of maggots, you haven't lived...and I hope you never do! There is also a sound that goes along with the feeding of that many maggots. Add the smell and you have the perfect combination for what nightmares are made of. If I haven't grossed you out enough by now, somebody has to pick that body up and put it into a body bag. If they are left decomposing long enough, bodies begin to liquefy. It makes for a tricky removal sometimes, as body parts fall off and maggots drop on to your shoes. I have great respect for coroners after doing this work. They ultimately have to deal with bodies until they are finally disposed of. Some are definitely more unpleasant to deal with than others.

You may remember in the introduction that I said the dead freak me out, but not the way you think. Now you know what I am referring to. For some people, they get desensitized to dealing with dead bodies in various stages of decomposition or in various states of injury from the manner in which they died. For me, after seeing hundreds of dead people, I still don't like it. I can't help but look into their eyes and see some kind of expression on their face, even those who've have their head torn off. That is one of the creepiest things I've had to deal with. As I have mentioned, the dead have a certain smell, a certain look and a certain feel, and they freak me out!

Perhaps the most demented type of crimes that have had the most negative impact on me are violent sexual assaults on children. It is one of the most personal and emotionally destructive crimes there is. An adult sex offense is bad enough, but it is a thousand times worse when it happens to a child. In most cases, children can't defend themselves and are often trusting of their attackers. For the purpose of this book, I will not go into detail, but I will say, I was not emotionally prepared for my first sexual assault investigation.

It was the rape of a five-year-old girl. In cases like these, we have specially trained forensic interviewers assigned to talk with the children, and we observe the interview on a big screen TV in a room across the hall. The room is child friendly, full of bright colors, toys, bean bags, etc., to try and create an area of comfort and happiness. What information usually comes out of that room, in most cases, is not child friendly, comforting, or happy by any extent. In this particular incident, the interviewer began her dialog with the little girl. It started out very casual and pleasant at first, like most interviews do, but then went downhill really fast. After listening to this little girl describe, in great detail, what she had gone through, and hearing such vulgar language come out of such a small person as she repeated what her attacker said to her as he raped her, I was crushed. I was not prepared to hear expletives from a child that young as she was expressing the words of her attacker and I was certainly not prepared to hear what physically was done to her and to know the pain she had gone through.

An assigned worker from children's services and the female medical doctor who were sitting in the room with me both had tears in their eyes, as I'm sure I did, but I had a job to do and had to maintain my composure. After all, I'm the big tough Detective, right?

When the interview was over, I went to my car, stunned from what I just heard, and broke down. It was the first time I was emotionally hit that hard and it left me sick to my stomach and, honestly, I was pissed off. I have never shared that story with anyone until now, not even my wife who will be only be learning about it here, as she reads this for the first time, but it was too difficult to talk about at the time.

Lauren was aware that I was on my way to the interview and that I had a difficult time with it afterwards, but my emotions were just not something I could talk about, nor did I want to bear the sorrow I had for that little girl on anyone else. Lauren was there for me just the same and I didn't really have to tell her anything. She is my peace and my comfort and I am grateful for her just being there when I need her the most!

So, when I am asked if I have ever been scared on a paranormal investigation, or by ghosts, or something evil, my answer is always a resounding no. I have never seen more anger, more fear, more evil, or such a complete lack of compassion for another human being during anything that I have ever done on any paranormal investigation, anywhere, than I have seen involving the living, and it saddens me tremendously to know that there are people out there who just don't care. Compared to the horrific acts of violence that the living often inflict upon the living, including many attempts on me personally, it's almost funny to be asked if I have ever been scared by a ghost, because they don't even come close in comparison. I wonder why we're not more scared of the living, yet we're so afraid of ghosts.

Sure, there are paranormal cases where some people report being assaulted, scratched, pushed or scared, but no one has ever been killed by a ghost. Their fear is coming from inside themselves based on what they think a ghost is, or not knowing what it is, why it's there or what it wants. For those paranormal cases where people report being sexually assaulted or attacked in some manner, I have observed that there is always something that the living person has done, is doing, or was part of something that someone else has done, that created the situation in the first place. Call them possessions if you want, but I look at it as a conflict with the person's own personal demons, which are strictly there because of them. They created the situation that allowed whatever is going on to happen. Many people may disagree with me and that is fine, but from my point of view, it is still the living that must take the responsibility for the activity and to largely work on the cure for their problem themselves, rather than looking to outside resources. However, I know people have many different views on ghosts, many different reactions and ways they deal with them and I respect each and every perspective and opinion.

I have worked on many police investigations where I have been pushed, kicked, and scratched by the bad guys. I have had a pistol pointed at me, knives pulled on me, and someone tried to run me over with a car. I have been cursed at, have had things thrown at me, and had to look at humans in various forms of disfigurement and death.

My partners have been my own personal therapists because they understand what I have gone through, and I have been theirs. Just a few weeks before I sat down to write this chapter, one of my partners told me that he couldn't wait to retire. He had just come back from a suicide investigation involving a man who shot himself in the head. It was a bloody scene and my partner commented that he is tired of having to see brains and blood dripping from the ceiling and then having to go home an hour later and pretend that the world is perfect for the sake of his three young children. The fact of the matter is, we do that all the time. I ask you to remember, after getting a little inside look at a very small portion of the downside of police work, whether you hate the police or love them, if you have to deal with a police officer for a personal issue or as a result of being pulled over in your car, they are ultimately there to help you and the community as a whole. Before you make any harsh judgment of them, please keep in mind that you don't know what they may have had to go through earlier that day, or maybe the night before, because of someone else's doing.

Chapter 16
You Stole My Ghost

If you think about all the cruel and destructive ways that people behave, it's easy to see how they should be feared more than ghosts. Through the many years of verifiable insights given to me by psychic mediums, I have also come to realize that if ghosts do remain, many of them can be just as compassionate and understanding as the living can be. You don't see these dramatic, and sometimes beautiful, stories behind hauntings on TV because they just don't sell, as I have been told by many producers. I've tried many times to create a program to convey those types of haunting stories, however, most television producers are not interested. If it's not scary or otherwise wild and crazy in some sensational manner, nobody's interested in airing it. Apparently, the people pulling the strings behind the networks want you to be scared instead of telling you the whole truth. The truth is, I have been a part of some very emotional, compassionate, and surprisingly loving hauntings.

Over the years, I have had the pleasure of meeting many people and listening to their concerns and claims of activity. Some people are scared and want whatever it is that is in their house or business out, but others are completely okay with the activity and considers the spirit to be a part of their family. That is a good thing because sometimes it is their family who is there. I have been on cases where our medium has tracked the spirit down and identified them as a former homeowner, and grandmother.

After the new family moved in, the spirit would make frequent checks on the children as they lay in bed at night. There was only a loving and protective intent from the side of the spirit, but the family just knew that someone was invading the sanctity of their children's bedroom and they were frightened that their children would be hurt.

I have also been a part of many cases where former homeowners remained at their home because that's where they derived the most love from when they were alive and couldn't bear to leave. Some spirits become very attached to their homes. Many people are very protective of their homes as well, and want to make sure it is taken care of. When the family is maintaining the house to the satisfaction of the spirit, often times the spirit will take on a protective role to the residents, as well as the home itself.

If you remember the three-hundred-year-old home that my team had investigated which I spoke of earlier, the former homeowner loved the house so much and recognized that the new owner felt the same way, so she wanted to stick around to be a part of the new owner's life and support her in any way she could from the other side. The mediums I've worked with have told me about spouses that can't bear to leave their significant others and remain in a home after their death until the passing of their spouse. They then move on together. We have worked many cases like that. I'm reminded of a case where a four-year-old son in a family was killed in a car accident. He stuck around with his family after his death and, when a close family friend died soon after, he stayed behind to care for the little boy until the little boy was ready to move on. In another case, I asked the spirit of a seven-year-old girl to jump on the bed to see if I could see anything physical happening. Our medium told me that the girl was waving her finger and saying no... no... no, and relating that the mom currently residing in the home does not allow anyone to jump on the bed. When we checked with the mom, she told us that jumping on the bed was forbidden in their home because her daughter almost died when she fell off the bed one day and struck her head on the dresser. She stopped breathing for a few seconds, but came around. Amazingly, the young spirit recognized this rule and obeyed the mom's wishes. I found this to be one of the most remarkable interactions I've ever heard of between a spirit and the living.

There are endless reasons why a spirit would stick around after dying and endless ways that they can interact with the living. I have seen an outstanding number of supernatural occurrences in my time studying the paranormal, heard about a few bad spirits here and there through our mediums, but most spirits were reported to be good people in bad situations who decided to stay, for one reason or another, after they died. It's a very personal thing to decide if you believe if ghosts are real or not. Some people have one profound experience and they're convinced they've seen a ghost, while others need repetitive events to happen before they will concede. Some people remain skeptical and will never believe, no matter what they witness.

For me, it wasn't something I could hear about, read about, or watch on TV to sway me in my beliefs. I am a spiritual person, and even somewhat religious, but I never really bought into everything my church, or any church, for that matter, was telling me. I found some of what people were telling me to be just plain wrong, in my opinion, and much of it contradictory, in some respects. I mean no disrespect to any faith or church. This was just the way I perceived things for myself. The fact that I like to know things for myself, rather than rely on what other people tell me, was a big factor in my beliefs, as well. I personally believe that I, and everyone else, can be directly connected to God, whatever God that is for you, if there is a God. I don't want to rely on a middleman who may or may not even believe his own words. But enough about God, as that's an entirely different book. The bottom line is that direct experience has always been the way for me.

One of my most profound experiences, while working with The PPA, was an investigation we conducted at a restaurant in Lake Ariel, Pennsylvania. It was a typical case for all intents and purposes. Virginia picked up on the spirit of a former property owner and provided details about his personality and day to day practices, which the clients were able to confirm with great amazement. This case would soon manifest the biggest and most convincing experience for me out of all the cases I have been a part of. After years of conducting many investigations, in various locations, with never having seen a fully manifested ghost before, I would soon come to the realization of what it is that I believe about ghosts today.

Actually, when I think about it more thoroughly, I still haven't seen a fully manifested ghost! Anyway, at the conclusion of a very comprehensive physical investigation, Virginia was ready to try and release the spirit of the former property owner. Knowing that I had been taught some techniques with Reiki energy work for cleansing spaces, Virginia had asked me to go and sit in the middle of the dining room and do some energy work. This also entailed a great deal of visualization and, in the metaphysical world, thought is energy and energy creates change. Virginia had gathered the remaining team members at a table on the far side of the room, away from where I was working. Virginia would say a few prayers and try to connect with the spirit. This was pretty typical for a case, so up until then, things were fairly routine. Once Virginia begins her work, she does not like to be interrupted because it hurts her energy and can break a connection with a spirit. I began to do what Virginia had requested of me, but finished long before she had, so I sat quietly by myself for a few minutes. One thing I noticed after working so many resolution cases is that sometimes Virginia is successful at helping a spirit into the light very quickly and other times it takes a while. It really depends on the spirit she is working with and the fact that we believe that every person, living or dead, has free will. If they don't want to go, that is a choice they make. Virginia sometimes has to "talk" with a spirit for a while before they are ready to let go and move on. When we're lucky, they are ready to go before we are ready to release them.

As I sat listening to Virginia, she was telling the team that she was having a little bit of trouble with the spirit not wanting to go. Twiddling my thumbs and not really doing anything, I figured it was a good time to see what else I could accomplish for myself with the help of my guides and angels, and see if they were listening. I didn't know what to do, so I just closed my eyes and took a few deep breaths to relax and quiet my mind a little bit. Next, I called to my guides and angels in a very general way and just said to them that, if they were with me and if there was anything I could do to help the people in this restaurant, please guide me to accomplish that. With nothing happening, I had an idea pop into my mind, or maybe that idea was something happening, I'm not sure! Either way, I thought back over the many reoccurring tornado dreams I've had for a few years. Why tornadoes? If you figure it out, please let me know! They have sometimes been small, or big and powerful, depending on the dream, but never hurt anyone. They reminded me, as I sat there, how Virginia often describes columns of swirling light that spirits ascend into as they move on to wherever it is they go. Why not give that a try, I thought. I envisioned a sparkling, swirling column of white and gold light, much like the tornados in my dream, coming down from the sky and into the room, swirling around in one spot. I then imagined a door, opening at the base with the intent that the spirit could leave through that opening if he chose to.

Still with nothing happening, I thought for a minute and had another idea from a technique that we've used in the past. Again, in a general way, I asked of my guides and angels that if there was anyone on the other side that knew this man and who could come for him, please have them come and meet him at the door in the column of light. I envisioned a few people popping into the doorway in a very happy way and waving their hands, as if to say hello. It was at that moment that chills ran up my spine like nothing I've ever felt before and I became very cold inside. I've felt a few cold spots on prior cases and have had the occasional chills like most people have experienced, but nothing like this. I was cold on the inside, like I had been outside for a few hours on a frigid winter's day, but that's not even the weird part. It was just a few seconds after the onset of the chills that it happened. I'm not even sure exactly what it was that happened, but before I knew what was going on,

I had an overwhelming sensation that something had wrapped itself around me. That is the only way I can describe what it felt like. Something was on me! It was such a strong sensation that my heart was pounding and I was just about to yell out to Virginia, but I held myself back.

She really doesn't like to be interrupted, so I didn't want to be the cause of her having to try to reconnect with a spirit after she had been working with him for a few minutes already, or have her throw something at me. So, back to my brains I went, trying to figure out what else I could do to follow this through. Something was going on, I started it, and it was now up to me to take care of it. But how do I do that? More visualization, I supposed.

In my mind, I slowly expanded the size of the tornado, making it bigger and bigger, until it finally was right in front of me. With nothing happening still, I figured I would expand the vortex to completely engulf me. The moment the outside wall of the tornado touched me, I literally felt something peel right off of me and saw it in my mind, a darker shade of something coming right off and into the vortex. That was not part of my visualization! I was concentrating on making the vortex bigger, but that image just popped in there all on its own. As soon as whatever it was seemed to come off of me, I immediately warmed up and the chills were gone. Believe it or not, that's still not the crazy part! From across the room, I could hear Virginia, in a very excited and confused voice, exclaiming to the team, "Where'd he go? I was just talking to him! He was just here! Where'd he go?"

"Um, Virginia!" I uttered in a shaky voice. "I think I need to tell you something."

I explained to Virginia what I had just done and what I had gone through. Virginia told me that the guy was just standing next to her, right there, as she pointed to a spot on the floor. The team at the table related that Virginia had been talking to the guy and he seemed to have just disappeared. I told Virginia that I could actually feel something wrap around me, what I had done to remove it, and that I actually felt it go. Virginia had a bit of a stunned look upon her face and her only response to me at that time was, "Holy shit, you stole my ghost!" I guess I did, but never in a million years would I have thought that was possible.

Chapter 17
Grow Your Mind

It's hard not to believe in ghosts when you have just released one. When I experienced whatever it was that
I experienced that night, it changed me. Virginia congratulated me on the release of a spirit and told me
that is exactly what she does in some cases to help get
spirits across to the other side. I have never experienced
anything like that in the many years that I have been
investigating the paranormal. It's one thing to have
a physical sensation while doing some visualization
work, but to have it affect another unwitting person,
and to have it confirmed by a person who I trust wholeheartedly and who had no idea what I was up to, was
outstanding, to say the least. It most certainly gave me
some things to reflect upon afterwards.

So, how do you decide if ghosts are real? Any way
you need to! It was a very long process for me, but a
necessary one. When I look back at my involvement in
the metaphysical and paranormal fields, from my first
meeting with Sue, all the way up to present day, I now
understand it was all a learning process for me. Some
people are lucky and see a ghost right off the bat, while
for others, including me, it has been a long journey.

When people tell me that they have never seen a ghost but would really like to, I always respond by telling them to be patient. It's just like watching for a shooting star. If you look long enough, you're eventually going to see one. I have spent many years trying to uncover my truth about ghosts, most often feeling like I was just chasing shadows, but I've had some incredible experiences along the way. I've been involved in hundreds of investigations and have yet to see a ghost with the clarity or detail that Lauren or Jim have described. I, on the other hand, have seen more physical activity than any other person on our team. I often think that maybe we're not the ones in control of when or where we see a ghost. Maybe we're allowed to see a ghost at certain stages in our lives for a particular purpose, whatever that purpose may be. I have seen, by far, too much over a long period of time not to acknowledge that ghosts are real. I have moved beyond a "Preponderance of the Evidence" to "Beyond a Reasonable Doubt," which means there is sufficient evidence, along with testimony, to win a criminal court case.

If we were to examine all of the witnesses who have had encounters with ghosts, we'd have to go back a long way. Thousands of years, in fact! People have been reporting ghost encounters for a very long time and they don't seem to be going away, either. From a scientific perspective, in this stage of human evolution, when we are more intelligent than ever, we should be finding more logical explanations for ghost encounters. Yet, the belief in ghosts still remains and reports of encounters seem to be increasing. Why is this? The perception doesn't seem to be affected by societal intelligence levels, whether an individual is highly intelligent or has a diminished capacity, what they are witnessing is still perceived as a ghost. If we look at the witnesses who have requested help from my team alone, you will find that they aren't crazy lunatics. Ok, well, maybe one or two, however, with the exception of those individuals who have not been diagnosed with any mental disorders, what we find is a variety of ordinary people, just like you and me. My team has helped blue collar families, white collar families, doctors, dentists, school bus drivers, professors, police officers, mayors and other governmental workers, photographers, business owners, and so many more. We have investigated mobile homes, mansions, police stations, office buildings, theaters, ... I think you get my point!

There is no particular type of person or personality reporting issues with ghosts. There is no specific age group, ethnic background, or religion. Nearly every conceivable class or group you can place a person into has reported seeing ghosts. Even very young children, who can barely speak and who have no concept of what a ghost is, report seeing them. Infants and toddlers make up a very large portion of the people who witness spirits firsthand. The witness list is long, the majority is credible and most would certainly hold up in a court of law.

What every court of law likes to see, which also backs up witness testimony, is evidence. There are literally thousands of paranormal teams popping up around the country and around the world. Some are very simple, hobby based groups who enjoy getting together just to experience the thrill of witnessing paranormal activity, while others are hard core scientific researchers conducting very intricate experiments. There are also a million varieties in between. The fact is, even though some of the evidence that comes out of a few groups may be questionable, every team, great or small, is able to document some type of evidence at some point, and some of it is pretty amazing. There are several scientific researchers that have shared some of their incredible findings on environmental changes as precursors to a paranormal event occurring. These findings have been reproducible, adding to their validity. Changes that are commonly found to occur immediately prior to an event include such things as an increase in positive or negative ions at the event site, a burst of gamma radiation, a spike in the Electromagnetic Field (EMF), or a drop in barometric pressure, to name just a few. These are very easily measured and very well documented pieces of information that go far beyond the use of old fashioned dowsing rods to search for ghosts. For those people looking for concrete evidence of paranormal activity, these are just a few things to look at as paranormal events occur. We can't directly measure the energy of a ghost, but we can identify certain precursors to manifestations or the presence of a ghost with some certainty.

When you take into account psychic impressions to identify the cause of a haunting, you have to consider the validity and accuracy of that information. I have been studying psychic mediums for nearly twenty years and have become very proficient at testing them under a variety of conditions. When I am working a case, I am always asking the medium to tell me where the activity is occurring, what type of activity is manifesting and what, or who, is causing it. To go one step further, I compare those impressions with historical facts obtained through team research and from the clients' personal knowledge of the history of the location and the people located there. It is very hard to discount accurate information from a credible psychic medium when that information is consistently confirmed, and in the cases I have done with them, it has been.

The more information a jury has available to them to make an informed decision about a crime, the better capable they will be of doing so. For the paranormal investigations I have been involved in, I have always maintained that a comprehensive, investigative approach was the best way to look at all aspects of a haunting. You have to include all available sources of information in order to make the best possible conclusion. Over the past eight years of actively investigating paranormal hotspots, homes, and businesses, I have come to my own personal conclusion that ghosts are real, based on the totality of the circumstances and years of studying this phenomenon. There is just too much evidence, too many witnesses, and a never-ending supply of investigation requests for it to be any other way. There will always be a great number of people who will be skeptical or who will never believe, but those people are on their own path and must live in their own reality. Perhaps they are just not ready to see what is out there beyond the physical world.

To those who are skeptical or non-believers, but are, at the same time, religious, I offer this brief anecdote. A few years ago, I had a conversation with a friend who claimed that he did not believe in ghosts. I had shared some of my personal experiences with him that I have had over the years, but he told me he just did not believe in them. I commented that I did not realize that he was an atheist, but that was okay with me, as I was not trying to convince him. The term "Atheist" did not sit well with him and he corrected me and explained that he was not an atheist, he believed in God and that we go to heaven or hell when we die. I asked him by what means do we get there. His answer was that our soul goes there somehow. I asked him what he meant by "our soul." He said our spiritual being, the part of us that is left after we die, he guessed. I asked him if he meant that we exist outside of a living, physical body in some other form.

That was a hard question to answer, but he assumed so. I then asked him to look at what he had just described to me and tell me the difference between what he just described and a ghost. His answer was that he was always taught that we either go to heaven or hell, there is no in-between. That didn't answer the question and, the fact was, he just unknowingly admitted that he believed in ghosts, however existing somewhere other than here. So, where is heaven and how do we get to this magical place? Can there be an in-between and, if so, what is between here and there if Heaven is somewhere else? We know the physical world is far from perfect, so couldn't we get stuck just outside of heaven's reach on occasion? Isn't there even a smidgen of a possibility that we just don't know for sure, or do we know for sure? Have we just been told what is or isn't possible, so we choose to believe because someone said it was that way? If God truly does exist and gave us free will, do we have the choice to either stay when we die or ascend to a much higher level of being, or even go somewhere else?

To the skeptics and non-believers I say, you are not a true or informed skeptic, or non-believer, unless you put in a considerable amount of time investigating these issues for yourself in order to make a reasonable decision based on your research. Stop making conclusions based on what you've been told or what you've been taught by someone else who has probably not done any research themselves. You are not a real skeptic or non-believer until you can spend years in this field talking to witnesses, studying psychic abilities, and working on hauntings to come to the conclusion based on your findings, or lack of findings, whatever the case may be. If you then come to the conclusion that you do not believe, then you will at least have some ground to stand on. It's time to turn off the TV, put down the books, get out there yourself, and grow your mind!

There is a very well-known passage from the Lord's Prayer in the Christian faith that begins, "Our Father, who art in Heaven, Hallowed be thy Name. Thy kingdom come. Thy will be done, On Earth as it is in Heaven." If you look at where we come from based on these few words from the start of the Lord's Prayer, we might surmise that we come from the place where our "Father" exists, call it Heaven or whatever you will. "Thy will be done on Earth as it is in Heaven" may tell us that Heaven is the superior level of reality and that we are to do what is done there. From this prayer, we may conclude that we are sent here, from there, the place of our creator, where we have been created to be born into this reality.

For those of you who believe in ghosts and those of you who believe, or can at least admit, that we may come from a place where our creator is from, only to return there on some level after we die, I pose this question to you.

If we are created and sent here from there,
a non-physical reality to a physical reality,
born out of the non-physical,
but living in the physical,
and you see a ghost here in the physical reality,
a place that has been "created" for you,
the question is not, "Are ghosts for real,"
but rather, are you?

Acknowledgments and Final Thoughts

I've had so many great experiences and have met so many wonderful people through this journey. I truly believe that if I came out of it with no more answers than when I started, it would still have all been worth it.

Beginning years ago with Sue, the first psychic medium that I had the pleasure of meeting, all the way up to working full time today with VirginiaRose Centrillo, resident psychic medium at The PPA, I had an incredible learning experience and spiritual enlightenment that I would have never anticipated happening when I started. Tara, the tarot card reader, once told Lauren that if we started our group, it would be far greater than we could ever imagine, and it has been. Jack Olmeda, Michelle Gallagher, Lauri Moore, Robyne Marie, and so many other incredible psychic mediums helped our group along the way, and me personally on so many levels, that I will forever be grateful to all of them.

I certainly could not have accomplished anything without the help of the entire PPA family. The goal of creating a resolution based group was to ultimately help people while learning from each other. The hard work, dedication, and compassion that each member has shown for our clients through every investigation was amazing and I am a better person from having the experience of knowing each of them. They are the reason that The PPA has been so successful. The only thing better than going through something really weird, is going through it with friends. We have all become much more than friends, we are a close-knit family! I look forward to many more years of working together, easing the fears of the living, and moving the departed forward so that they may each evolve as unique souls as intended.

Chris B., a television producer from New York, recognized the extraordinary and sometimes unusual work of The PPA. I would like to express my sincere gratitude to Chris B., the entire production company, and the executives at Discovery Communications for your trust in The PPA and including us as reoccurring cast members on *The Haunted*. It was one of my most memorable experiences and gave our team the opportunity to let viewers see that a haunting can be most often resolved and that not every haunting has a bad intention behind it.

With so many paranormal "reality" shows being aired, and some being really far out there, it was a desire of mine to create a forum that I could talk about the true "reality" behind the hauntings, along with many other metaphysical and supernatural topics to bring people back down to earth. The common theme television and Hollywood were pumping out is that all hauntings are scary. That doesn't have to be our truth. It is only what we are programmed to think from repetitive viewing. When you can step back just for a moment and realize that what you are witnessing when you see a ghost is a truly incredible thing, you can turn that fear into faith; the faith that life goes on when we die. You are witnessing life after death! Somehow, somewhere, our soul goes on!

Nancy Kman, the Programming Director from WILK News Radio in the Scranton/Wilkes-Barre, PA area, put her trust in Lauren and me and offered us a spot on their weekend talk show lineup. We created a program called *Paranormal Science* where all the supernatural, paranormal, metaphysical, and holistic topics were discussed. This gave us the opportunity to look at many out of the ordinary topics in an open and objective manner. It also provided a forum for specialists in those fields to voice their opinions and perspectives to the listeners and enlighten us on their professions. During the first year, Nancy joined us as a co-host on the show and when we switched from a pre-recorded show to a live format in 2013, The PPA's Joe Hawk and Stan Zurek joined me as the co-hosts where we still appear every Sunday night at 8pm EST. The show has opened up many more doors and new adventures for our team and has been a great experience for me just to be a part of.

One door that opened for me was by a survivor of a very malevolent haunting. Chris Di Cesare was the victim of a 1985 haunting at the SUNY Geneseo College Campus in New York. It was a very well documented haunting that was later turned into an independent film entitled, *Please, Talk with Me*, directed by Mara Katria. Chris was asked to be a consultant on the film to protect the integrity of the events that occurred and his involvement would result in our later meeting and becoming friends. After connecting through a social media site, Chris learned of my involvement with a paranormal radio show that I hosted. After many conversations surrounding our mutual involvement in the paranormal, Chris invited me to MC a symposium for the film, prior to its premier, and I graciously accepted with great honor. I was happy to be involved in the promotion of PTWM because of the integrity of the film makers to keep it authentic by including Chris in the film's development and for the compassion they showed throughout the story—not only for the victim of the haunting, but in the end, for the haunter as well.

PTWM was later followed by a second film called *Surviving Evidence* and was written by Mr. Di Cesare himself. Chris and Mara asked for me to participate as a primary actor in the film opposite the lead character. My intended part was to be a police detective trying to get to the bottom of the haunting once and for all and pick it apart for authenticity. I guess I fit the part! Words cannot express how honored I was to be thought for this role. If you remember back to Chapter 1, I mentioned having my experience of hearing a voice while cutting grass when I was twelve years old. That experience was used as part of the script for my character in the film. The making of this film was yet another incredible learning experience and, once again, I had a chance to meet so many wonderful people involved in the paranormal community. Many people who were involved in the film, I later invited on to the radio show to talk with about their particular paranormal backgrounds.

During my down time on the set of *Surviving Evidence*, I had the opportunity to meet and talk with a great guy by the name of Chip Reichenthal. He was genuinely one of the nicest and most kindhearted people that I have ever had the pleasure of meeting. After just a few minutes of speaking with him, I recognized that Chip possessed a brilliant mind and an incredible way of looking at life. Chip would turn it all around though, to make me feel like the special one in the conversation, which was part of his brilliance. This wasn't unique to just me. I watched as Chip spoke with many other people and noticed that he had an amazing way of looking at people and honoring what makes each of those people individually special. He is a person who I am proud to say that I have become great friends with. Something that Chip had mentioned to me during our first meeting was that he had a special gratitude for police officers and especially those that also work in the paranormal field. Chip asked me if I would be a guest on his radio show, *Beyond the Norm with Chip Reichenthal*, at some point in the future and I told him that I would be happy to.

When the interview finally occurred, I was blown away once more with the honor and respect that was given to people in law enforcement through the wonderful tribute that Chip provided during the course of his show. I was truly touched and thankful on behalf of all men and women in law enforcement everywhere. There are many things that the public doesn't understand about police work or the things that police officers must go through and Chip wanted to honor those moments and give thanks to those selfless people. For this, I will be forever grateful.

Many months later, I received a phone call from Chip asking me if I would take a look at something he was working on and check it for accuracy against how real law enforcement officers work and communicate. It was a chapter for a book he was writing. Chip told me that he had included a character in the book that was a detective and he wanted to make sure the dialog was correct for public interaction by a detective. I gave Chip my feedback and he promised me a signed copy when it was released. I later received that signed copy as promised but, what Chip didn't tell me before, was that the detective was based on me. I was once again humbled and honored and proud to be a part of such a great project.

The book is called *Even the Dead Won't Tell You the Truth*. I know I'm partial, but the book is an excellent read and came at a very difficult time in my life. Reading the book actually got me through some difficult personal moments by taking my mind off of reality for a while as I submerged myself into a terrific murder mystery with a psychic twist. I definitely recommend that you check out his book. The universe was giving me many hints to write my own book and I actually had several people tell me flat out to get it started. I sometimes felt that I was being guided to write it but it wasn't until I went through the process of proof reading the few chapters of Chip's book that he allowed me to read, and then eagerly awaiting and finally seeing the outcome of the story, that I felt inspired to create something of my own to see what the outcome would be for me.

My wife, Lauren, who I affectionately refer to as "The Word Nazi" because of her wonderful editing skills, offered to preliminarily edit the manuscript for me and there was nothing holding me back. I wanted to share my experiences with people because I felt that I was just like so many others who've always wondered about ghosts and hauntings, but who didn't have the advantage of being able to go out and investigate like I did. The only way for me to know was to go find out for myself, so I did. It is really Lauren that I owe so much thanks and appreciation to for making all of this possible by sacrificing personal time together when she couldn't be with me. I give that same appreciation to my beautiful children, Nadine, Emma, and Marissa who had to sacrifice much of their time with me as well.

My mother, Arlene Keyes, has always been my biggest fan in everything I've done and had taught me to think for myself, be open-minded, and above all, be compassionate towards everyone, even the dead. She gave so much of her own time, to give me more time of my own, to pursue what I was so passionate about doing—investigating! She left us in May of 2014 at the young age of 68, but has made several appearances to VirginiaRose, coming through for me, and again, I've had more amazing experiences hearing Virginia relate so many events from my youth that I shared with my mother. I miss her dearly!

The PPA has become a second full time job for me because we receive so many requests for help. It is time consuming but extremely rewarding in the end. Every case is a learning experience for the team and I thank all of the clients who have put their trust in us over the years. I sincerely hope we made a difference in their lives because they have made a difference in ours.

It is a crazy thing, this paranormal world that surrounds us. I have been able to witness so many incredible things through this work, things that you usually only read about or see on TV. For me, it is real. I recently received an email from a young viewer who had watched a few episodes of *The Haunted*. He had a simple question for the group, "Are the ghosts who are talked about on the TV show real?" *Wow*, I thought, *that boy is me!* I have ended up being the exact same thing on TV that I questioned myself years ago, to someone else. I hope someday that young man reads this book and remembers that he is the one who sent that question in to The PPA because I want to thank him for a great reality check of my own. It was the first and only time I received an email with that particular question. My answer to the young man was this.

"I have been involved in this field of investigation for many years now. I have seen things that only a very small percentage of the population has experienced. I have worked with police officers, scientists, skeptics, psychic mediums, energy workers, close friends, and family. I have had the pleasure of working with my wife, Lauren, whose opinion I trust wholeheartedly. We have all had our own personal experiences of varying degrees and fall back on our faith, teachings, and beliefs to try and answer that same exact question ourselves. When I put all my faith, teachings, and prior beliefs aside and just look at what I have discovered for myself, I can honestly say, I believe they are real."

To the wonderful person sitting there right now reading this book, I ask that you take into consideration all of the things that I have shared with you through my experiences, but don't only take my word for it because your personal truth may be different than mine and I will honor that if so. There is a great journey that awaits you. If you want to know if ghosts are real, it's up to you to figure out for yourself anyway. Go find out! Until then, keep this in mind; it really doesn't matter if you believe in ghosts or not, because they believe in you!

To learn more about The PPA,
visit our website: www.theppa.net

CPSIA information can be obtained
at www.ICGtesting.com
Printed in the USA
BVHW071357180819
556130BV00002B/171/P